The Thames Path

NATIONAL TRAIL

Companion

supported by

Countryside Agency

(Countryside Commission up to 1 April 1999)

1st edition published February 1999

© National Trails Office

ISBN 0–9535207–0–6

edited by Jos Joslin & Alison Muldal

Photographs on pages 30, 34/35, 36, 38, 41, 43, 44, 46, 52, 60, 61, 62, 77, 88, 97, 98, 106, 107, 109, 111, 114, 119, 120, 121, 122 top, 127, 128, and 129 by Rob Fraser;

Photographs on the cover and pages 2, 7, 14, 16, 32, 33, 48, 50/51, 55, 64, 69, 74/75, 82/83, 85, 91, 93, 94, 99, 100 and bottom of page 122 by Jos Joslin

Published by National Trails Office

Countryside Service

Cultural Services

Holton

Oxford OX33 1QQ

tel 01865 810224

fax 01865 810207

email mail@rway-tpath.demon.co.uk

website www.nationaltrails.gov.uk

Produced by Leap Frog Communications Ltd, Leeds

Designed by David Aldred

CONTENTS

INTRODUCTION

Welcome to this first Thames Path Companion. It provides up-to-date practical information about accommodation, refreshments and many other facilities along the 294 km of National Trail from the source of the river in Gloucestershire, through Wiltshire, Oxfordshire, Berkshire, Buckinghamshire, Surrey and into London. The Companion is designed to help with planning anything from a week's walking holiday to an afternoon out with the dog.

The Companion is not a route guide: for detailed information of the Trail itself, The Thames Path National Trail Guide by David Sharp (Aurum Press, 2nd reprint with corrections 1997 and 3rd due 1999, £12.99) is available from most book shops. Alternatively it can be mail ordered from the National Trails Office (see page 13 for details). The Companion complements the Trail Guide and, armed with a copy of each, it is hoped that anyone using the Trail needn't require anything more. Enjoy your trip.

Opened in 1996 as one of thirteen National Trails in England, the Thames Path follows the country's best known river for 294 km as it meanders from its source in the Cotswolds through several rural counties and on into the heart of London. This Trail provides level, easy walking and can be enjoyed in many ways, whether for an afternoon's stroll, a weekend's break or a full scale, but relatively gentle trek of its whole length. Another advantage of the Thames Path is that it is easy to reach by public transport, including an excellent network of train services the whole distance between Oxford and London.

At the start of the Path, the source of the River Thames beneath an elderly ash tree in a field in the Cotswolds, you may well find no water at all. However, gradually as you travel the trickle becomes a stream and soon a river bordered by willows and alders. As far as Oxford, apart from a couple of small historic towns and a few pleasant villages, there is a real sense of remoteness and rural tranquillity as the Thames winds its way through flat water meadows grazed by cattle or sheep, or fields of crops.

i Introduction

Beyond Oxford, the city of dreaming spires, you will still be in the heart of the countryside with its wealth of wildlife. The river whose banks you're following continues to widen, the willows seem to grow larger, and settlements become more frequent. From Goring where the Path coincides for a short distance with another National Trail, the ancient Ridgeway, the Chiltern Hills provide a wooded backdrop to your journey with their colours changing dramatically with the seasons.

When you reach Henley the Path starts to get busier with more people enjoying strolls with a dog, picnics on the bank or boating trips on the water. However, once you're away from towns or villages around a bend or two of the river, you'll regain the rural peacefulness. As the Thames Path passes beneath Windsor Castle, you are reminded that you are following a Royal river; the palaces of Hampton Court and Kew a little further downstream confirm this.

From the last non tidal lock on the Thames at Teddington, you can choose to walk on either the north or the south bank of the river through most of London. You'll pass leafy Richmond and Kew, remarkably green areas, before entering the heart of the City with its many famous buildings bordering the Thames. The final few kilometres to the finish at the Thames Barrier take you amongst restored warehouses and the working wharves in London's Docklands.

With the support of the Countryside Commission, the Thames Path is managed to the highest standards necessary for one of the most important paths in the country by the local highway authorities with a small dedicated team of staff.

HISTORY

The Thames Valley was originally settled by prehistoric people with the earliest occupations discovered so far dating from the New Stone Age, some 6 000 years ago. These are at Runnymede and Staines near the Thames, not far from present day London. The river has been a very important trading route for hundreds of years and it is really only during the latter half of the twentieth century that it has mostly ceased to carry goods. Nowadays leisure boats rather than barges are the main users of the Thames. It was in medieval times that the river became increasingly important for trade, especially in those days for carrying wool from the lush Cotswold meadows to London.

St Paul's Cathedral is built of Taynton stone quarried in the Cotswolds and carried to London by barges towed by men and horses from Radcot. By the 18th century London was the world's busiest port and Reading, for example, received 95% of its goods by barge towed along the River Thames.

The towpath between Lechlade and Putney, along which much of the Thames Path now travels, was established towards the end of the 18th century by the Thames Commissioners at a time when the country's new canal system was being built which connected the Thames to other parts of Britain. It was a difficult task since many landowners refused permission for the towing path to enter their land or there were natural obstacles in its way. As a result in many places the towpath switched from one bank of the river to the other and ferries were used to transfer the towing horses across the river. When the commercial traffic died as a result of competition from the railways so did the navigation ferries.

This created a major problem for the setting up of the Thames Path. Either bridges had to be built where the old ferries used to operate or alternative routes to the towpath had to be found.

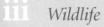

WILDLIFE

Wherever you walk along the Thames Path there should be plenty of wildlife to observe and enjoy although, of course, the time of year you are there is important. There will be birds present all year round, but if you're keen on wild flowers then April to September is the time to visit, and if insects are an interest of yours choose June to September.

Plants of the riverside seem to be especially colourful from the bright yellow of the flag iris and marsh marigold in spring to the pinks of the willowherbs and purple loosestrife during summer. Plants of particular note along the Path are the nationally rare Loddon lily and snake's-head fritillary, both flowering on a few flood meadows in early spring.

Insects are in abundance during the summer when dragonflies and damselflies, amongst the largest and so most noticeable, are active. There are various species, many wonderfully coloured and you'll be able to watch them mating, laying eggs, hunting for food or patrolling their territories.

Dragonfly photo: Matt Ball

Of the mammals you'll no doubt see rabbits and maybe a stoat or a weasel. Unfortunately you're unlikely to see a relative of the latter, an otter, although thankfully they are returning to the upper reaches of the Thames and perhaps in the future will be more plentiful and obvious. Another animal in trouble is the water vole, 'Ratty' of Kenneth Grahame's 'Wind in the Willows'. They used to be very common on the Thames emerging from their holes in the bank and busily ploughing backwards and forwards across the river, but their numbers have crashed in recent years. Let us know if and where you spot one.

The most obvious animals are the birds, many of which being water birds are large and thankfully don't fly away as soon as you appear! The majestic mute swan has to be the symbol of the Thames and is increasingly common thanks to the ban in the 1980s on anglers using lead weights. Swans eating these weights in mistake for the grit they need to take in to break down plant material in their gizzards were poisoned and killed and their numbers diminished considerably.

Wherever you go you'll see the commonest of Britain's ducks, the mallard, which like all ducks is especially resplendent from October to March. But other species of ducks visit the river too, so look out for tufted duck, pochard and wigeon. Geese, larger relatives of ducks, also abound in places, usually found in large noisy flocks grazing in fields near the river or roosting on the water itself. The Canada goose is very common.

USING THE THAMES PATH

The Thames Path is intended as a route for use by walkers, although parts, especially in towns and cities and near London, are designated for use by cyclists also. In a few places horseriders, too, can share the Path.

Spring, summer and autumn months are the best time to enjoy the Thames Path since there is very little risk of the river flooding and making the Trail impassable.

Whenever venturing into the countryside it is wise to be prepared for the elements: even in summer, wind and rain can make a walk cold and uncomfortable, so suitable warm and waterproof clothing should be worn or carried in a small rucksack. After rain, and particularly during winter, the Trail can be muddy, so wear strong, comfortable and waterproof footwear.

During winter months after heavy rain, some sections of the Path, especially in the upper reaches, can become flooded and unwalkable. To be sure of keeping your feet dry telephone the **Environment Agency's flood information line on 0645 881188.**

 ## DOG MATTERS

If you are planning to undertake a long distance walk along the Thames Path with your dog, you are advised to ensure it is fit before you start; on occasions walkers have had to abandon a walk because their dogs can't keep up!

Please also make sure your dog is under close control at all times to prevent it from disturbing livestock or wildlife. Whilst in fields with livestock you are asked to keep your dog on a lead, although on occasions cattle may harass you because of the dog and in such circumstances it may be wise to let it off.

FINDING YOUR WAY

Signing

The Thames Path follows a series of well-signed public rights of way along which people have a legal right of access.

An acorn, the symbol of Britain's National Trails, is used to guide your journey by marking the route in a variety of ways. It is used in conjunction with coloured arrows or the words 'footpath', 'bridleway' or 'byway' to indicate who can use a particular right of way.

The word 'footpath' and/or a yellow arrow indicates a path for use by walkers only and where, without the landowner's permission, it is illegal to cycle, ride a horse or drive a vehicle. Outside London, 83% of the Thames Path is footpath.

The word 'bridleway' and/or a blue arrow indicates a path which can be used by walkers, horseriders and cyclists but where, without the landowner's permission, it is illegal to drive any vehicle. Outside London, 6% of the Thames Path is bridleway.

The word 'byway' and/or a red arrow indicates a right of way which can be legally used by walkers, horseriders, cyclists and motorists. Outside London, 0.7% of the Thames Path is byway.

The Thames Path is signposted where it crosses roads and many rights of way using wooden or metal signposts. Elsewhere, waymark discs with acorns and coloured arrows are used on gates, stiles and waymark posts.

Finding Your Way

Guides

The Thames Path National Trail Guide by David Sharp, Aurum Press, 2nd reprint with corrections 1997 and 3rd due early 1999, £12.99 – the official Guide with written route description and colour maps.

Maps

It is always a good idea to use an Ordnance Survey map when walking, particularly in unfamiliar areas. The National Trail Guide includes colour sections of all the appropriate 1:25 000 maps needed to follow the Thames Path. Alternatively, for you to enjoy and interpret the wider landscape, you may wish to purchase your own maps.

The Landranger series (pink cover at 1:50 000 or 2 cm to 1 km) has all public rights of way, viewpoints, tourist information and selected places of interest marked on them. For the whole of the Path you will need:

163   Cheltenham & Cirencester
164   Oxford
175   Reading and Windsor
174   Newbury and Wantage
176   West London
177   East London

The larger scale new Explorer series (orange cover at 1:25 000 or 4 cm to 1 km) has more detail including fence lines which can be very helpful when following rights of way, recreational routes and greater tourist information. For the whole of the Path you will need:

168   Stroud, Tetbury and Malmesbury
169   Cirencester and Swindon
170   Abingdon, Wantage and Vale of White Horse (due January 1999)
180   Oxford (due January 1999)
171   Chiltern Hills West (due Spring 1999)*
172   Chiltern Hills East (due Spring 1999)*
160   Windsor, Weybridge and Bracknell
161   London South (due January 1999)
173   London North (due January 1999)

*Until Spring 1999 these are covered by Explorer 3, Chiltern Hills South

For those people with the old Pathfinder series (green cover at
1:25 000 or 4 cm to 1 km) for the whole of the Path you will need:

1133 (ST89/99)   Nailsworth & Tetbury
1134 (SU09/19)   Cricklade
1135 (SU29/39)   Faringdon
1115 (SP20/30)   Witney (South) & Carterton
1116 (SP40/50)   Oxford
1092 (SP41/51)   Woodstock
1136 (SU49/59)   Abingdon
1137 (SU69/79)   Watlington & Stokenchurch
1156 (SU68/78)   Henley-on-Thames & Wallingford
1155 (SU48/58)   Wantage (East) and Didcot (South)
1171 (SU47/57)   Hermitage & Chieveley
1172 (SU67/77)   Reading
1157 (SU88/98)   Maidenhead & Marlow
1173 (SU87/97)   Windsor
1174 (TQ07/17)   Staines, Heathrow Airport & Richmond
1190 (TQ06/16)   Weybridge, Esher & Hampton Court
1175 (TQ27/37)   Wimbledon & Dulwich
1159 (TQ28/38)   City of London
1176 (TQ47/57)   Bexley & Dartford

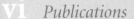

PUBLICATIONS ABOUT THE THAMES PATH

There are many publications available about the River Thames and its Path of which the following is a selection:

The Thames Path National Trail Guide by David Sharp, Aurum Press, 2nd reprint with corrections 1997 and 3rd due early 1999, £12.99 – the official Guide with written route description and colour maps.

The Thames Path by Leigh Hatts, Cicerone Press, 1998

Pub Walks along the Thames Path – 20 Circular Walks by Leigh Hatts, Countryside Books 1997

Rambling for Pleasure along the Thames East Berkshire Ramblers Group

Walks along The Thames Path by Leigh Hatts, Patrick Stephens Ltd, 1990

Chilterns and Thames Valley Walks Ordnance Survey Pathfinder Guide, 1994

Thames: the river and the path GEO Projects, 1996 - a fold-out map at a scale of 1:60 000.

Arcadian Thames by Mavis Batey, Henrietta Buttery, David Lambert and Kim Wilkie, Barn Elms Publishing, 1994.

Victorians on the Thames by R S Bolland, Midas Books, 1974.

A Guide to London's Riverside by Suzanne Ebel and Doreen Impey, Constable, 1985.

The Book of the Thames by Alan Jenkins, Macmillan London, 1983.

The Secret Thames by Duncan Mackay, Ebury Press/Countryside Commission, 1996.

The Ordnance Survey Guide to the River Thames (Series Editor, David Perrott), Nicholson Publications, 1984 (with frequent revisions).

Thames Crossings by Geoffrey Phillips, David & Charles, 1981

A Thames Companion by Mari Pritchard and Humphrey Carpenter, Oxford Illustrated Press, 1975.

London River by Gavin Weightman, Collins & Brown, 1990.

USEFUL CONTACTS

Thames Path Manager

National Trails Officer, National Trails Office, Cultural Services, Holton, Oxford OX33 1QQ. Tel: 01865 810224. Fax: 01865 810207. Email: mail@rway-tpath.demon.co.uk

Highway Authorities responsible for public rights of way

Buckinghamshire County Council, Environmental Services Dept, County Hall, Walton Street, AYLESBURY HP20 1UY. Telephone 01296 395000.

Gloucestershire County Council, Environment Dept, Shire Hall, Westgate Street, GLOUCESTER GL1 2TH. Telephone 01452 425535.

Oxfordshire County Council, Countryside Service, Cultural Services, Holton, OXFORD OX33 1QQ. Telephone 01865 810226.

Reading Borough Council, Leisure Services, Civic Offices, Civic Centre, READING RG1 7TD. Telephone 01189 390900.

Royal Borough of Windsor and Maidenhead, c/o Babtie Public Services Division, Shire Hall, Shinfield Park, READING RG2 9XG. Telephone 0118 987 5444.

Surrey County Council, Environment, County Hall, KINGSTON KT1 2DY. Telephone 0181 541 9343.

Swindon Borough Council, Borough Engineers Dept, Premier House, Station Road, SWINDON SN1 1TZ. Telephone 01793 463000

West Berkshire Council, c/o Babtie Public Services Division, Shire Hall, Shinfield Park, READING RG2 9XG. Telephone 0118 987 5444

Wiltshire County Council, Dept of Environmental Services, County Hall, TROWBRIDGE, Wilts BA14 8JD. Telephone 01225 713000

Wokingham District Council, Environment Services, Shute End Offices, WOKINGHAM RG40 1GY. Telephone 01189 778731.

Agency responsible for National Trails

Countryside Commission, South East Regional Office, 71 Kingsway, London WC2B 6ST. Tel: 0171 8313510.

Agency responsible for the River Thames

Environment Agency, Kings Meadow House, Kings Meadow Road, Reading RG1 8DQ. Tel: 0118 953500.

Environment Agency's Flood Information. Tel: 0645 881188

Weather Call (up-to-date weather forecasts)

0891 772275	Section One (Wiltshire and Gloucestershire)
0891 772276	Sections Two, Three, Four and Five (Oxfordshire, Berkshire and Buckinghamshire)
0891 772272	Section Six (Surrey)
0891 772271	Sections Seven and Eight (London)

GETTING THERE

The Thames Path is exceptionally well served by public transport which makes it possible to explore the Trail without needing a car by using trains, buses or, unusually for a National Trail, boats.

A free leaflet summarising the bus, train and boat services to the Trail is available from the National Trails Office (see page 13 for details)

Thames Trains operating trains between London, Reading and Oxford stopping at a further eight stations close to the Path (Tilehurst, Pangbourne, Goring, Cholsey, Culham, and Radley and the branch lines from Maidenhead and Twyford) issues a special ticket for walkers. Ask for a Thames Path Cheap Day Return ticket to the furthest point of your walk and it covers you automatically for the return journey on the same day from another Thames Trains station.

A summary of useful telephone numbers for public transport for the whole Trail is listed here although unfortunately not quite all areas have an enquiry line. Information about train services is included in each of the eight sections but bus information is not since services can change very frequently – if details were listed in this guide they would quickly be out of date and irrelevant.

- National Rail *all sections* -   24 hours a day 0345 484950
- Section One -   Gloucestershire County Council
01452 425543
Wiltshire County Council
0345 090899
- Sections Two, Three, Four   Oxfordshire County Council
and Five -   01865 810405

- Section Five -   Buckinghamshire County Council
                          0345 382000

- Sections Six and Seven - Surrey County Council 01737 223000

- Sections Seven and Eight - London Transport Travel Information
                          0171 222 1234

                          web: www.londontransport.co.uk

                          boat trips: 0839 123 432

RESPECT THE COUNTRYSIDE

• Enjoy the countryside, but remember that most of the Thames Path crosses private farmland and estates which are living and working landscapes.

• Always keep to the Path to avoid trespass and use gates and stiles to negotiate fences and hedges.

• Crops and animals are the farmer's livelihood – please leave them alone.

• To avoid injury or distress to farm animals and wildlife, keep your dogs under close control at all times – preferably on a lead through fields with farm animals (NB if you are concerned that cattle are harassing you, it may be safer to let your dog off the lead)

• Remember to leave things as they are – fasten those gates you find closed. Straying farm animals can cause damage and inconvenience.

• Please take your litter home, otherwise it can injure people and animals and looks unsightly.

• Guard against all risk of fires especially in dry weather.

• Take special care on country roads and, if travelling by car, park sensibly so as not to obstruct others or gateways.

Emergency Contacts

In emergency dial 999 and ask for the service required.

Police

To contact local police stations, telephone the number relevant to the section/county you are in and ask to be put through to the nearest police station.

Section	County	Tel Number
One	Gloucestershire	01242 521321
	Wiltshire	01793 528111
Two	Gloucestershire	01242 521321
	Oxfordshire	01865 846000
Three	Oxfordshire	01865 846000
Four	Oxfordshire & Berkshire	01865 846000
Five	Berkshire & Buckinghamshire	01865 846000
Six	Berkshire	01865 846000
	Surrey	01483 571212
	Thames River Police (from Staines Bridge to Teddington)	0171 928 0333
Seven	Surrey	01483 571212
	Greater London	0171 230 1212
	Thames River Police	0171 928 0333
Eight	Greater London	0171 230 1212
	Thames River Police	0171 928 0333

Hospitals

The following hospital with casualty departments are located in the places shown below. The telephone numbers given are for the hospital switchboard; ask to be put through to Accident & Emergency Reception.

* Full 24-hour emergency service
† Minor injuries only, 24-hour service

Section	Town/City	Telephone No	Address
One	*Cirencester	01285 655711	Cirencester Hospital, the Querns, Tetbury Road, Cirencester
	*Swindon	01793 536231	Princess Margaret Hospital, Okus Road, Swindon.
Two	*Swindon	01793 536231	Princess Margaret Hospital, Okus Road, Swindon.
	*Oxford	01865 741166	John Radcliffe Hospital, Headley Way, Headington, Oxford
Three	*Oxford	01865 741166	John Radcliffe Hospital, Headley Way, Headington, Oxford
	†Wallingford	01491 835533	Wallingford Community Hospital, Reading Way, Wallingford
Four	†Wallingford	01491 835533	Wallingford Community Hospital, Reading Way, Wallingford
	*Reading	0118 987 5111	The Royal Berkshire Hospital, London Road, Reading
	†Henley	01491 572544	Townlands Hospital, York Rd, Henley

X *Emergency Contacts*

Five	†Henley	01491 572544	Townlands Hospital, York Road, Henley
	*High Wycombe	01494 526161	Wycombe General Hospital, Queen Alexandra Road, High Wycombe
Six	*Slough	01753 633000	Wexham Park Hospital, Wexham Street, Slough
	*Chertsey	01932 872000	St Peter's Hospital, Guildford Road, Chertsey
	*Kingston upon Thames	0181 546 7711	Kingston Hospital, Galsworthy Road, Kingston upon Thames
Seven	*Isleworth	0181 560 2121	West Middlesex Hospital, Twickenham Road, Isleworth
	*Hammersmith	0181 846 1234	Charing Cross Hospital, Fulham Palace Road, London W6
	*Chelsea	0181 746 8000	Chelsea & Westminster Hospital, Fulham Road, London SW6
Eight	*Lambeth	0171 928 9292	St Thomas Hospital, Lambeth Palace Road London SE1
	*The City	0171 955 5000	Guy's Hospital, St Thomas Street London SE1
	*Dartford	01322 227242	Joyce Green Hospital Joyce Green Lane, Dartford

TOURIST INFORMATION CENTRES

If you are unable to find accommodation using the entries in this guide, local Tourist Information Centres may be able to help. They are found in the following places.

*Offers accommodation booking service for personal callers during opening hours.

*Cirencester	Corn Hall, Market Place, Cirencester GL7 2NW. Tel 01285 654180, fax 01285 641182
Opening hours	Summer: (Apr-end Dec) Mon 9:45-17:30, Tue-Sat 9:30-17:30 Winter: (Jan-end Mar) Mon 9:45-17:00, Tue-Sat 9:30-17:00
*Swindon	37 Regent Street, Swindon SN1 1JL. Tel 01793 530328, fax 01793 434031
Opening hours	All year: Mon-Sat 9:30-17:30
*Faringdon	Market Place, Faringdon SN7 7HL. Tel/fax 01367 242191
Opening hours	Summer: (Easter-Oct 31) Mon-Fri 10:00-13:00, 13:30-17:00, Sat 10:00-13:00 Winter: (Nov 1-Easter) Mon-Sat 10:00-13:00
*Witney	Town Hall, Market Square, Witney OX8 6AG, tel 01993 775802, fax 01993 709261
Opening hours	Summer: (Apr 1-Oct 31) Mon-Sat 9:30-17:30 Winter: (Nov 1-Mar 31) Mon-Sat 10:00-16:30
*Oxford	The Old School, Gloucester Green, Oxford OX1 2DA. Tel 01865 726871, fax 01865 240261
Opening hours	Summer: (Easter-Sep 30) Mon-Sat 9:30-17:00, Sun 10:00-15:30. Winter: (Oct 1-Easter) Mon-Sat 9:30-17:00. Bank Holidays 10:00-15:30
*Abingdon	25 Bridge Street, Abingdon OX14 3HN. Tel 01235 522711, fax 01235 535245
Opening hours	Summer: (Apr 1-Oct 31) Mon-Sat 10:00-17:00, Sun 13:30-16:15 Winter: (Nov 1-31 Mar) Mon-Fri 10:00-16:00, Sat 9:30-14:30

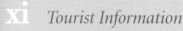

*Wallingford	Town Hall, Market Place, Wallingford OX10 0EG. Tel 01491 826972, fax 01491 825844
Opening hours	All year: Mon-Sat 10:00-16:00
*Reading	Town Hall, Blagrave Street, Reading RG1 1QH. Tel 0118 956 6226, fax 0118 939 9885
Opening hours	All year: Mon-Fri 10:00-17:00, Sat 10:00-16:00
*Henley-on-Thames	Town Hall, Market Place, Henley-on-Thames RG9 2AQ. Tel 01491 578034, fax 01491 411766
Opening hours	Summer: (Mar 31-Sep 30) daily 10:00-19:00 Winter: (Oct 1-Mar 31) daily 10:00-16:00
*Marlow	31 High Street, Marlow SL7 1AU. Tel 01628 483597, fax 01628 471915
Opening hours	Summer: (Easter-Sep 30) Mon-Fri 9:00-17:00, Sat 9:30-16:30, Sun 10:00-16:30 Winter: (Oct 1-Easter) Mon-Fri 9:00-17:00, Sat 9:30-16:30
*Maidenhead	The Library, St Ives Road, Maidenhead SL6 1QU. Tel/fax 01628 781110
Opening hours	All year: Mon, Tue, Thu, Fri 9:30-17:00, Sat 9:30-16:00
*Windsor	24 High Street, Windsor SL4 1LH. Tel 01753 743900 (general information) 01753 743907 (accommodation bookings), fax 01753 743904.
Opening hours	Mon-Sun 10:00-17:00 (subject to seasonal changes)
Kingston upon Thames	Market House, Market Place, Kingston upon Thames KT1 1JS. Tel 0181 547 5592, fax 0181 547 5594, web site www.rbk.kingston.gov.uk.
Opening hours	All year: Mon-Fri 10:00-17:00, Sat 9:00-16:00

*Richmond	Old Town Hall, Whittaker Avenue, Richmond TW9 1TP. Tel 0181 940 9125, fax 0181 940 6899.
Opening hours	Summer: (May 1-Oct 31) Mon-Fri 10:00-18:00, Sat 10:00-17:00, Sun 10:15-16:15. Winter: (Nov 1-Apr 30) Mon-Fri 10:00-18:00, Sat 10:00-17:00
*Britain Visitor Centre	1 Lower Regent Street, London SW1 4XT (personal callers only).
Opening hours	All year: Mon-Fri 9:00-18:30, Sat-Sun 10:00-16:00
*London Tourist Board	Victoria Station (personal callers only). For accommodation bookings: Tel 0171 932 2020 'Credit Card Booking Service' – no general enquiries.

City of London Information Centre

	St Paul's Churchyard, London EC4M 8BX. Tel 0171 332 1456, fax 0171 332 1457 (no accommodation information).
Opening hours	Summer: (Apr 1-Sep 30) daily 9:30-17:00 Winter: (Oct 1-Mar 31) Mon-Fri 9:30-17:00, Sat 9:30-12:30
*Southwark	Lower Level, Cotton's Centre, Middle Yard, London SE1 2QJ. Tel 0171 403 8299 (situated in Hay's Galleria).
Opening hours	All year: daily 10:00-17:00
*Greenwich	46 Greenwich Church Street, Greenwich, London SE10 9BL. Tel 0181 858 6376, fax 0181 853 4607
Opening hours	Daily 10:00-17:00 (subject to seasonal changes).

Other Tourist Information Centres

Other tourist information centres are located at: Heathrow Airport (Terminal 3 Arrivals Concourse and Heathrow Underground Station Concourse), Liverpool Street Underground Station, Selfridges (Basement Services Arcade), Waterloo International Station.

ACCOMMODATION, FACILITIES & SERVICES

This booklet gives details of the settlements, accommodation, eating places, shops, attractions and other facilities along the Thames Path. They are listed in geographic order from the source of the river to the Thames Barrier in London. Under each settlement campsites and youth hostels are listed at the end.

If you fail to find accommodation using this guide please contact the Tourist Information Centres which may be able to provide other addresses. Some towns near London, and London itself, have such an extensive range and number of places to stay that details of individual establishments are not listed in this guide.

The Thames Path is divided into eight sections as indicated on the map on page 1. At the start of each section is a map showing the settlements close to the Trail within that section. These maps are meant only as a guide and you are recommended to use this Companion in conjunction with The Thames Path National Trail Guide or Ordnance Survey maps.

You are strongly advised to book accommodation in advance, and during summer as early as possible. Whilst booking, do check prices since those quoted here are usually the minimum charged.

For those who would like to walk the Thames Path without having to carry all their possessions, quite a few accommodation providers have indicated whether they are willing to transport the luggage you don't need during the day to your next night's accommodation. The fee charged for this service needs to be discussed and agreed at the time of the booking. Accommodation providers have also indicated if they are willing to collect you from the Thames Path and deliver you back after your stay.

All the information within this Companion is as accurate as possible. Inclusion of accommodation does not constitute a recommendation although it is indicated in the details whether an establishment has a recognised grade awarded by the English Tourist Board, AA or RAC. If you have any comments or notice any errors, please write to Jos Joslin the National Trails Officer (see page 13 for details).

KEYS TO SYMBOLS FOR SETTLEMENTS AND ACCOMMODATION

Settlement

Comments relate to preceding icon.

map grid reference (see introduction to each section for relevant maps)

shortest walking distance from Thames Path

nearest railway station

pubs (usually open daily 11am-3pm then 6pm-11pm)

✗ bar meals

✉ post office (usually open daily 9am-5.30pm weekdays; closed 12.30pm Sat)

general store (usually open daily 9am-5.30pm Mon-Sat)

opening hours for general stores

S M T W T F S

For example: full day opening   half day opening   full day closing

cafe/tea shop

£ banks (usually open daily 9.30am – 4.30pm Monday to Friday)

cash machine

☎ telephone

toilets

police station

Tourist Information Centre

Accommodation

Prices quoted are minimum price per person per night for bed and breakfast, whether in a single, double or twin room.

🛏	double room	🚿	showers
🛏	single room	🚻	toilets
🛏	twin room	⊡	laundry facilities
🛏	family room	🏪	site shop
🚭	no smoking	ETB	English Tourist Board
DRY	clothes drying facilities	AA	Automobile Association
🔥	packed lunches available	RAC	Royal Automobile Club
🍴	evening meals available at accommodation or locally	👑	ETB grading for hotels, B&Bs, inns and guesthouses
V	caters for vegetarians	✓	ETB grading for campsites, caravan parks
👫	children welcome		
🐕	dogs allowed by arrangement	★	AA, RAC grading for hotels
🎁	luggage transported to next overnight stop by arrangement	Q	AA grading for B&Bs
		LI	ETB/AA listed
🚗	transport to and from Trail by arrangement	AP	ETB approved
		CO	ETB commended
♿	wheelchair access	HC	ETB highly commended
⛺	tent pitches	DL	ETB de luxe
🚐	caravan pitches	AC	RAC acclaimed
🚰	hot water	HA	RAC highly acclaimed
🚰	cold water		

The Source to Lechlade

Section One

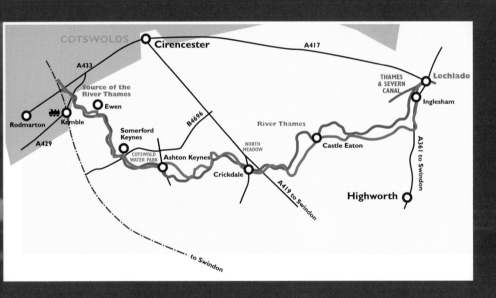

1 The Source to Lechlade

This rural first 37 km of the Thames Path is within the fine countryside of the Cotswolds where farming and small village communities dominate. The river you follow grows from nothing to a trickle to a respectable body of water by the time you reach Lechlade.

1 *A Taster*

The source of the Thames at the start of this section lies in a remote Gloucestershire meadow beneath the boughs of an elderly ash tree. For much of the year this spring is dry and, especially if you're walking during the summer, you may find the bed of the Thames remains without water for some distance.

Your route following the infant river wanders through fields and through or near to several small Cotswold villages characterised by creamy stonework buildings with stone slate roofs. These are ideal places to enjoy a refreshment stop.

Before you reach the small, originally Saxon, town of Cricklade where the right of upstream navigation ends, you'll pass through the middle of the Cotswold Water Park and its blue landscape of gravel extracted lagoons. Just outside Cricklade the Path skirts around the edge of North Meadow where, usually towards the end of April, the rare snake's-head fritillary flowers in vast numbers.

At Inglesham the flow of the Thames is increased by the water of the River Coln which joins it. The church and Round House here are worth seeing before you walk on into Lechlade.

Landranger Maps	Explorer Maps	Pathfinder Maps
163 Cheltenham & Gloucester	168 Stroud, Tetbury & Malmesbury 169 Cirencester & Swindon 170 Abingdon, Wantage and Vale of White Horse	1133 (ST89/99) Nailsworth and Tetbury 1134 (SU09/19) Cricklade 1135 (SU29/39) Faringdon

Public Transport Information

- National Rail - 24 hours a day   0345 484950
- Gloucestershire County Council   01452 425543
- Wiltshire County Council   0345 090899

Police

Gloucestershire 01242 521 321   Wiltshire 01793 528111

Hospitals

Cirencester 01285 655711
Cirencester Hospital, the Querns, Tetbury Road, Cirencester
Swindon 01793 536231
Princess Margaret Hospital, Okus Road, Swindon

TOURIST INFORMATION CENTRES

Cirencester	Corn Hall, Market Place, Cirencester GL7 2NW. Tel 01285 654180, fax 01285 641182
Opening hours	Summer: (Apr-end Dec) Mon 9:45-17:30, Tue-Sat 9:30-17:30 Winter: (Jan-end Mar) Mon 9:45-17:00, Tue-Sat 9:30-17:00
Swindon	37 Regent Street, Swindon SN1 1JL. Tel 01793 530328, fax 01793 434031
Opening hours	All year: Mon-Sat 9:30-17:30

1 The Source to Lechlade

CIRENCESTER

SP0201 ⌂ On the Path Town
with full range of services
🚂 Kemble 8km ℹ️

Sunset

Mrs J Castle
Sunset
Baunton Lane
CIRENCESTER GL7 2NQ
☎ 01285 654822

Apr-Oct 🛏️£14.50 🛏️ £14.50 🛏️2
🛏️ 1 V 🅰️🚫 👫 over 5 yrs 🚭 DRY
🚗 ⛽ ETB LI CO

The Golden Cross Inn

Mr & Mrs M Smith
The Golden Cross Inn
Black Jack Street
CIRENCESTER GL7 2AA
☎ 01285 652137

all year 🛏️£18.00 🛏️ £15.00 🛏️ 1
🛏️ 1 V 🅰️🚫 not Sat, Sun 👫 DRY
🚗 ⛽ ETB 👑

The Ivy House

Mrs J Marriott
The Ivy House
2 Victoria Road
CIRENCESTER GL7 1EN
☎ 01285 656626

all year 🛏️£28.00 🛏️ £20.00 🛏️3
🛏️ 1 V 🅰️🚫 👫 🚭 DRY

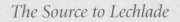

The Crown of Crucis Hotel

Mr R K Mills
The Crown of Crucis Hotel
Ampney Crucis
CIRENCESTER GL7 5RS
☎ 01285 851806
Fax 01285 851735

closed 24-30 Dec 🛏️£56.00 🛏️£41.00
🛏️8 🛏️17 **V** 🏠 🛎️ 🌂 🚻 ♿ **DRY**
AA ★★★ ETB 👑👑👑👑 **CO**

RODMARTON

 ST9497 🏞️ 3.5km
🚂 Kemble 6.8km ✉️

The Old Rectory

Mrs Fitzgerald
The Old Rectory
Rodmarton
CIRENCESTER GL7 6PE
☎ 01285 841246
Fax 01285 841246

closed Xmas, New Year 🛏️£25.00
🛏️£22.50 **V** 🚫 🌂 🚻 🚭 **DRY** 🚗 🎁
ETB 👑👑

KEMBLE

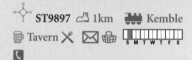

ST9897 ⌂ 1km 🚂 Kemble

🍺 Tavern ✕ ✉ 🧺 ▯▯▯▯▯▯▯
S M T W T F S

☎

Smerrill Barns

Mr Chris Benson
Smerrill Barns
Kemble
CIRENCESTER GL7 6BW
☎ 01285 770907
Fax 01285 770706

all year 🛏£38.00 🛏£24.00 🛏 1
🛏 4 🛏 1 🛏 1 V 🔥 🚫 🚭 **DRY** 🚗
ETB ♔♔♔ HC AA QQQQ

EWEN

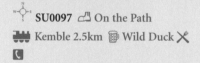

SU0097 ⌂ On the Path

🚂 Kemble 2.5km 🍺 Wild Duck ✕

☎

The Wild Duck Inn

Mr Gary Burton
The Wild Duck Inn
Ewen
CIRENCESTER GL7 6BY
☎ 01285 770310
Fax 01285 770924

all year 🛏£49.50 🛏£34.75 🛏 8
🛏 3 V 🚫 📺 ⛶ AA ★★ RAC ★★★

ASHTON KEYNES

SU0494 ◻ On the Path

🚋 Kemble 9.2km

🍺 Horse & Jockey ✕ White Hart ✕

Plough ✕ ✉ 🧺 ⑂|||||||||||||| ☎
  S M T W T F S

Corner Cottage

Mrs Rosina Wiltshire
Corner Cottage
Fore Street
Ashton Keynes
SWINDON SN6 6NP
☎ 01285 861454

Jan-Nov 🛏£25.00 🛏£18.50 🛏1
🛏 1 ⚠🚭 ♟ DRY ETB 👑👑 CO

Waterhay Farm

Mrs J Rumming
Waterhay Farm
Leigh
CRICKLADE
SN6 6QY
☎ 01285 861253

all year 🛏£25.00 🛏£21.00 🛏1
🛏1 V 🚭🚭 DRY ETB 👑👑 CO

Mrs V B Threlfall

1, Cove House
Park Place
Ashton Keynes
SWINDON SN6 6NS
☎ 01285 861226

all year 🛏️£30.00 🛏️£24.00 🛏️1
🚪1 V ⓥ 🚭 👫 🚫 DRY 🎁
ETB 👑 👑 HC

CRICKLADE

⊹ **SU0993** 🚶 On the Path
🚂 Swindon 12.5km 🍺 several ✕
✉️ 🧺 |S|M|T|W|T|F|S| ☕
£ Lloyds ▤ 📞 👫 🔔

Dolls House

Mrs Jemma Maraffi
Dolls House
The Street
Latton
CRICKLADE SN6 6DJ
☎ 01793 750384

all year 🛏️£16.00 🛏️£16.00 🛏️1
🛏️1 🚪1 V ⓥ 🖼️ 👫 DRY 🚗 🎁

Leighfield Lodge Farm

Mrs C Read
Leighfield Lodge Farm
CRICKLADE SN6 6RH
☎ 01666 860241
Fax 01666 860241

all year 🛏️£27.00 🛏️£22.00 🛏️1
🚪1 ⓥ 👫 🚫 DRY ETB 👑 👑 CO

Mrs P Shield

23 High Street
CRICKLADE SN6 6AP
☎ 01793 750205
Fax 01793 752010

closed Xmas, New Year 🛏️£19.00
🛏️£28.00 🛏️1 🛏️1 🚪1 V 🔖 ⓥ
🖼️ 👫 DRY 🚗 🎁

CASTLE EATON

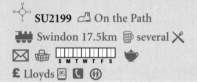

SU1495 🐾 On the Path
🚂 Swindon 13.8km 🍺 Red Lion ✗
not Mon lunch ✉ 📞

Second Chance Touring Park

Mrs B Stroud
Second Chance Touring Park
Marston Meysey
SWINDON SN6 6SZ
☎ 01285 810675

Mar-Nov 🛶 £7.00 ⛺ £5.00 🚐 26
⛺ 26 📖 🚿 🚻 ♿ Cross to north
bank at Castle Eaton

LECHLADE

SU2199 🐾 On the Path
🚂 Swindon 17.5km 🍺 several ✗
✉ 🧺 |||||||||| 🍵
          S M T W T F S
£ Lloyds 🖼 📞 ♿

Cambrai Lodge

Mr John Titchener
Cambrai Lodge
Oak Street
LECHLADE GL7 3AY
☎ 01367 253173

all year 🛏 £25.00 🛏 £19.00 🛏 2
🛏 1 🛏 1 V 🚲 🚫 🔲 🚻 🚫 ♿ **DRY**

The Plough Inn

Mr & Mrs T Pardoe
The Plough Inn
Kelmscot
LECHLADE GL7 3HG
☎ 01367 253543
Fax 01367 252514

closed 24-30 Dec 🛏 £30.00 🛏 £25.00
🛏 1 🛏 4 🛏 2 🛏 1 V 🚲 🚫 🔲 🚻
DRY 🚗

The New Inn Hotel

Mr Nick Sandhu
The New Inn Hotel
Market Square
LECHLADE GL7 3AB
☎ 01367 252296
Fax 01367 252315

all year 🛏️ £40.00 🛏️ £22.50 🛏️ 27
🛏️ 2 V 🔥 🅰️ 🏠 🚻 ♿ **DRY** 🚗 📦
ETB 👑👑👑

St John's Priory Park

The Proprietor
St John's Priory Park
Faringdon Road
LECHLADE GL7 3EZ
☎ 01367 252360

Mar-Oct 🚐 £5.00 ⛺ £4.00 🚐 25
⛺ 15 🅰️ 🔥 🔥 ❶ 🅰️ 📦
ETB ✓✓✓

Bridge House Camp Site

Mr R Cooper
Bridge House Camp Site
Bridge House
LECHLADE GL7 3AG
☎ 01367 252348

Mar-Oct 🚐 £3.50 ⛺ £3.50 🚐 6
⛺ 45 🅰️ 🔥 🔥 ❶ 🔄 🅰️ 📦 ♿ **DRY**

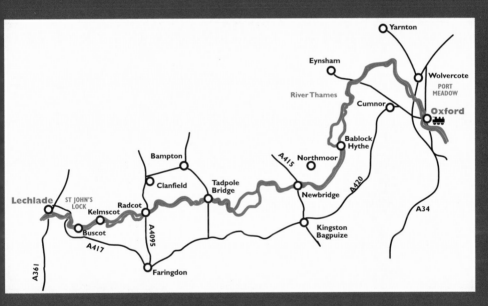

2 Lechlade to Oxford

This 50 km stretch is the most remote of the whole Trail. The Path follows the ever growing Thames as it slowly winds its way through the flat flood plain of the Thames Valley and you'll experience large skies and peaceful views. You'll rarely encounter settlements and will cross only a few, mostly minor, roads.

If you want peace and quiet more than anything, then this is the section of the Thames Path for you to explore. Once you leave Lechlade behind, and have paid your respects to Old Father Thames at St John's Lock, you'll be hard-pressed to find many farmsteads or villages close to the Path until you reach the outskirts of Oxford. Luckily, however, your walk will be interspersed with the occasional road crossing with a welcoming pub on the river bank, and at one crossing a choice of pubs, one on each bank!

Mixed farming and lots of sky dominate the landscape here. You'll walk through meadows grazed by sheep or cattle, many with hedges abundant with blackberries as long as you're there at the right time of year. Other fields are planted with a variety of crops, their colour changing with the seasons and influencing the views you'll enjoy.

The river grows broader all the time, its course frequently marked by tall willows or the shorter alders, both liking to have their roots in water. Unfortunately alders are starting to suffer from a fungal disease carried by water and in places are beginning to die.

Not far from Lechlade you'll pass close to the small village of Kelmscot and further on you should stop to look at the oldest bridge on the Thames at Radcot.

From Tenfoot Bridge to Shifford Lock the Path is still temporary and follows a rural route for about 3 km through Duxford whilst the lengthy legal work to create a footpath on the north bank of the river is completed. However, it is hoped that this work will be finished before long.

Landranger Maps	Explorer Maps	Pathfinder Maps
163 Cheltenham & Cirencester 164 Oxford	170 Abingdon, Wantage and Vale of White Horse 180 Oxford	1135 (SU29/39) Faringdon 1115 (SP20/30) Witney (South & Carterton) 1116 (SP40/50) Oxford 1092 (SP41/51) Woodstock

2 A Taster

Public Transport Information
- National Rail - 24 hours a day   0345 484950
- Oxfordshire County Council   01865 810405

Police
Gloucestershire 01242 521 321   Oxfordshire 01865 846000

Hospitals
Swindon 01793 536231
Princess Margaret Hospital, Okus Road, Swindon.
Oxford 01865 741166
John Radcliffe Hospital, Headley Way, Headington, Oxford

TOURIST INFORMATION CENTRES

Swindon   37 Regent Street, Swindon SN1 1JL.
                    Tel 01793 530328, fax 01793 434031
Opening hours   All year: Mon-Sat 9:30-17:30

Faringdon   Market Place, Faringdon SN7 7HL.
                    Tel/fax 01367 242191
Opening hours   Summer: (Easter-Oct 31) Mon-Fri 10:00-13:00,
                    13:30-17:00, Sat 10:00-13:00
                    Winter: (Nov 1-Easter) Mon-Sat 10:00-13:00

Witney   Town Hall, Market Square, Witney OX8 6AG,
                    tel 01993 775802, fax 01993 709261
Opening hours   Summer: (Apr 1-Oct 31) Mon-Sat 9:30-17:30
                    Winter: (Nov 1-Mar 31) Mon-Sat 10:00-16:30

Oxford   The Old School, Gloucester Green, Oxford OX1 2DA.
                    Tel 01865 726871, fax 01865 240261
Opening hours   Summer: (Easter-Sep 30) Mon-Sat 9:30-17:00,
                    Sun 10:00-15:30. Winter: (Oct 1-Easter) Mon-Sat
                    9:30-17:00. Bank Holidays 10:00-15:30

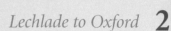

BUSCOT

SU2397 🥾 0.6km

🚂 Swindon 18km 📫

🧺 |S|M|T|W|T|F|S| 🫖 📞 ♿

Apple Tree House

Mrs Elizabeth Reay
Apple Tree House
Buscot Village
FARINGDON SN7 8DA
☎ 01367 252592

all year 🛏️ £23.00 🛏️ £18.00 🛏️ 2
🛏️ 1 V 🚶 🚭 👪 🚭 ETB 👑 👑

RADCOT

SU2899 🥾 On the Path

🚂 Swindon 24km 🍺 Swan Hotel 🍴

📞

The Swan Hotel

Mrs Sandra Fairall
The Swan Hotel
Radcot
BAMPTON OX18 2SX
☎ 01367 810220

Jan 6 – Dec 22 🛏️ £25.20 🛏️ £19.00
🛏️ 1 🛏️ 2 V **DRY**
🚐 £3.75 ⛺ £2.75 🚐 10 ⛺ 15
🚿 ♿ 🧺 🚭 *all year*

FARINGDON

⊕ **SU2895** ⌂ 4.5km Town with full range of services

🚂 Swindon 19.5km ℹ️

Sudbury House Hotel

Mr Andrew Ibbotson
Sudbury House Hotel
56 London Street
FARINGDON SN7 8AA
☎ 01367 241272
Fax 01367 242346
Email sudburyhouse@cix.co.uk

all year 🛏️£49.00 🛏️£29.50 🛏️10
🛏️39 🛏️2 V 🕭🕯️🚫🅿️🛆🚻 ♿ DRY
AA ★★★ RAC ★★★
ETB 👑👑👑👑

Faringdon Hotel

Mr Nizar Peera
Faringdon Hotel
1 Market Place
FARINGDON SN7 7HL
☎ 01367 240536
Fax 01367 243250

all year 🛏️£50.00 🛏️£37.50 🛏️3
🛏️13 🛏️1 🛏️3 V 🕯️🅿️🛆🚻
AA ★★ RAC ★★ ETB 👑👑👑

CLANFIELD

⊕ **SP2801** ⌂ 2.9km

🚂 Shipton 16km

🍺 Clanfield Tavern ✕ Plough ✕

✉️ 🧺 | | | | | | | | | | 🌙
      S M T W T F S

The Granary

Mrs Payne
The Granary
Clanfield
BAMPTON OX18 2SH
☎ 01367 810266

all year 🛏️£17.00 🛏️£17.00 🛏️1
🛏️1 🛏️1 V 🕭🚻🚫 DRY 🚗
ETB 👑👑👑 CO

The Plough at Clanfield

Mr John Hodges
The Plough at Clanfield
Bourton Road
Clanfield
BAMPTON OX18 2RB
☎ 01367 810222
Fax 01367 810596

all year 🛏️£65.00 🛏️£47.50 🛏️6 V
🕭🕯️🚻 over 12 yrs DRY 🎁
AA ★★★ RAC ★★★

BAMPTON

SP3103   3.6km

Oxford 29km   several ✕   ✉

S M T W T F S   £ Midland closed Wed 📞 ⓘ

Morar

Mrs Janet Rouse
Morar
Weald Street
BAMPTON OX18 2HL
☎ 01993 850162
Fax 01993 851738
Email morar@mcmail.com

Mar-mid Dec 🛏 £22.00 🛏 2 🛏 1
V 🔥 🚫 👫 over 6 yrs 🚭 DRY
ETB 👑👑 HC

The Talbot Hotel

Mr Adam Russell
The Talbot Hotel
Market Square
BAMPTON OX18 2HA
☎ 01993 850326
Fax 01993 850326

all year 🛏 £22.50 🛏 £17.50 🛏 2
🛏 2 🛏 2 V 🔥 🚫 🗝 👫 DRY 🚗 🔌
ETB 👑👑👑 AA **AP** RAC **AP**

2 Lechlade to Oxford

The Romany Inn

Mr Robert Smith
The Romany Inn
Bridge Street
BAMPTON OX18 2HA
☎ 01993 850237
Fax 01993 852133

all year 🛏£26.00 🛏£21.00 🛏2
🛏3 🛏2 🛏4 V 🖊🚫🖼🚹🏂
ETB 👑👑 **AP**

TADPOLE BRIDGE

✣ **SP3300** 👢 **On the Path**
🚂 Oxford 25km 🍺 Trout Inn ✕ 📞

The Trout Inn

Mr Chris Green
The Trout Inn
Tadpole Bridge
Buckland Marsh
FARINGDON SN7 8RF
☎ 01367 870382

all year 🚐 £4.00 ⛺ £3.00 🚐 15
⛺ 20 🚿🚿🏂🚫 not Sun during
winter 🖼♿

Rushey Lock

The Lock Keeper
Rushey Lock
Tadpole Bridge
Buckland Marsh
FARINGDON
☎ 01367 870218

Apr-Oct 5 🛁 ⊕ Available only to walkers and boaters

NEWBRIDGE

☼ SP4001 ◁ On the Path
🚂 Oxford 18.5km
🍺 Rose Revived ✕ Maybush ✕

The Rose Revived

Mr Andrew Jones
The Rose Revived
Newbridge
WITNEY OX8 7QD
☎ 01865 300221
Fax 01865 300115
Email andy@therose.demon.co.uk

all year 🛏 £42.50 🛏 £26.25 🛏 6
🛏 1 **V** 🗚 🚫 💼 🛉 🚻 ♿

KINGSTON BAGPUIZE WITH SOUTHMOOR

☼ SU4098 ◁ 3.5km
🚂 Oxford 15.5km
🍺 Hinds Head ✕
🧺   ☎

Foxside B&B

Mrs Sally Atkins
Foxside B&B
Sandy Lane
Kingston Bagpuize with Southmoor
ABINGDON OX13 5HX
☎ 01865 820693
Fax 01865 820034

all year 🛏 £20.00 🛏 £17.50 🛏 1
🛏 1 🛏 **V** 🚫 💼 🛉 🚻 🚭 ♿ **DRY**
🚗 ⛽

Alpenhaus

Mrs Pat Curtis
Alpenhaus
Faringdon Road
Kingston Bagpuize with Southmoor
ABINGDON OX13 5AF
☎ 01865 820666
Fax 01865 821868
Email Bbalpen@aol.com

all year 🛏️£25.00 🛏️£17.50 🛏️1
🚪2 🏊 🚫 👭 🚭 **DRY** 🚗

Fallowfields Country House Hotel

Mr & Mrs A J Lloyd
Fallowfields Country House Hotel
Kingston Bagpuize with Southmoor
ABINGDON OX13 5BH
☎ 01865 820416
Fax 01865 821275
Email stay@fallowfields.com

all year 🛏️£85.00 🛏️£52.50 🛏️7
🚪3 🚪2 V 🏊 🚫 🐾 👭 🚭 **DRY** 🚗
🎁

NORTHMOOR

✛ **SP4202** ⌂ 1.8km

🚂 Oxford 22.5km 🍺 Red Lion ✕

📞

The Patch

Mrs M C Gilbert
The Patch
Northmoor
WITNEY OX8 1AY
📞 01865 300684

Feb-Nov, Sun-Thu only 🛏£32.00
🛏 £22.00 🛏 1 🚿 1 **V** 🖋 🚫 ⊘
DRY 🚗

Rectory Farm

Mrs Mary Anne Florey
Rectory Farm
Northmoor
WITNEY OX8 1SX
📞 01865 300207
Fax 01865 300559

Feb-mid Dec 🛏£35.00 🛏 £22.50
🛏 1 🚿 1 **V** 🖋 🚫 ⊘ **DRY** 🚗 ETB
👑👑 HC

Northmoor Lock Field

The Lock Keeper
Northmoor Lock Field
c/o West Farm
Eaton
ABINGDON OX13 5PR
📞 01865 862908

Mar-Oct ⛺ 25 🚰

Lower Farm

Mrs Wade
Lower Farm
Northmoor
WITNEY OX8 1AU
📞 01865 300237

all year 🚐 £3.00 ⛺ £2.00 🚐 5
⛺ 5 🚰 🟢 not Mon

2   *Lechlade to Oxford*

BABLOCK HYTHE

SP4304 On the Path

Oxford 9.3km

Ferryman Inn ✗ Foot ferry across river during pub opening hours, weather permitting

The Ferryman Inn

Mr Peter Kelland
The Ferryman Inn
Bablock Hythe
Northmoor
WITNEY OX8 1BL
☎ 01865 880028
Fax 01865 881033

not Xmas, Boxing Day £40.00
£22.50 3 1 2 V ⚠ ⊘
♿ ⊘ ⚠ DRY ⊞ ETB ♔♔♔ CO

£7.50 £5.00 5 5
⚒ ⚒ ⊘ ♿ ⚠ ⊘ ⊞

CUMNOR

SP4603 3.5km Foot ferry across river from Bablock Hythe during pub opening hours, weather permitting

Oxford 5.4km

Bear & Ragged Staff ✗ Vine ✗
✉ 🛒 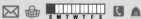 S M T W T F S ☎ ⚓

The Cumnor Hotel

Mrs Marilyn Maskell
The Cumnor Hotel
76 Abingdon Road
Cumnor
OXFORD OX2 9QW
☎ 01865 863098
Fax 01865 862217

all year £44.00 £29.50 1
4 1 1 V ⚠ ⊘ ☐ ♿ ⊘

EYNSHAM

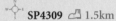 **SP4309** 1.5km

Coombe 7.5km several ✕

✉ 🛒 | | | | | | | | ☕
S M T W T F S

£ Barclays 📱 📞 ♿ 🔔

Swinford Park

Mrs Christine Tapper
Swinford Park
Swinford
Eynsham
WITNEY OX8 1BY
☎ 01865 881212

closed Xmas £18.00 £16.00 1
1 1 V ⚠ 🚫 ♟ 🚭 **DRY**

Pinkhill Lock

The Lock Keeper
Pinkhill Lock
Eynsham
WITNEY
☎ 01865 881452

all year 5 Available only to
walkers and boaters.

Eynsham Lock

The Lock Keeper
Eynsham Lock
Eynsham
WITNEY
☎ 01865 881324

all year 10 ♿ Available only
to walkers and boaters.

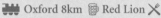

WOLVERCOTE

SP4809 △ 0.8km

🚂 Oxford 5.5km 🍺 Trout ✕

Red Lion ✕ Plough ✕ ✉

🧺 | S M T W T F S | 📞

Kings Lock

The Lock Keeper
Kings Lock
Wolvercote
OXFORD
☎ 01865 553403

all year ⛺ 10 🚰 Available only to
walkers and boaters.

YARNTON

SP4712 △ 4.5km **Cross river at
Kings Lock or Godstow Bridge**

🚂 Oxford 8km 🍺 Red Lion ✕

Grapes ✕ ✉ 📞

King's Bridge Guest House

Ms M Shaw
King's Bridge Guest House
Woodstock Road
Yarnton
KIDLINGTON OX5 1PH
☎ 01865 841748
Fax 01865 370215

closed Xmas 🛏 £35.00 🛏 £20.00
🛏 1 🛏 1 🛏 1 V 🥾 🚫 👫 🚭
ETB 👑👑 CO

OXFORD

✛ SP5106 On the Path **City**
with full range of services Oxford
ℹ️

Mrs R M Old
58 St John Street
OXFORD OX1 2LQ
☎ 01865 515454

all year £18.00 £18.00 1 1
1 ✷ ✷✷ DRY

White-House View

Mr G M Pulker
White-House View
9 White-House Road
OXFORD OX1 4PA
☎ 01865 721626

all year £23.00 £20.00 2
2 3 1 V ✷ ✷✷ ♿

Combermere House

Mr & Mrs Welding
Combermere House
11 Polstead Road
OXFORD OX2 6TW
☎ 01865 556971
Fax 01865 556971

all year £24.00 £20.00 4
1 4 V ✷✷✷ DRY 🚗 ⊞

Acorn Guest House

Mrs Nest Lewis
Acorn Guest House
260/262 Iffley Road
OXFORD OX4 1SE
☎ 01865 247998

closed Xmas, New Year £25.00
£19.00 4 4 1 3 V ✷
✷✷ over 9 yrs ♿ DRY
AA **Q** LI RAC **LI** ETB **LI** CO

Brown's Guest House

Mr & Mrs G McHugh
Brown's Guest House
281 Iffley Road
OXFORD OX4 4AQ
☎ 01865 246822
Fax 01865 246822
Email brownsgh@hotmail.com

all year 🛏£25.00 🛏£21.00 🛏4
🛏3 🛏3 🛏2 V 🪣 🚭 🛢 🛗 🚭
ETB **CO**

Bravalla Guest House

Ms Bernadette Downes
Bravalla Guest House
242 Iffley Road
OXFORD OX4 1SE
☎ 01865 241326
Fax 01865 250511

all year 🛏£25.00 🛏£20.00 🛏1
🛏3 🛏1 🛏1 V 🚭 🛢 🛗
AA **LI** RAC **LI** ETB **CO**

Sportsview Guest House

Mr & Mrs M S Saini
Sportsview Guest House
106-108 Abingdon Road
OXFORD OX1 4PX
☎ 01865 244268
Fax 01865 249270

all year 🛏£25.00 🛏£20.00 🛏6
🛏5 🛏4 🛏5 V 🚭 🛗
ETB 👑👑 **AP**

Cornerways Guest House

Mrs Carol Jeakings
Cornerways Guest House
282 Abingdon Road
OXFORD OX1 4TA
☎ 01865 240135
Email jeakings@btinternet.com

closed Xmas 🛏£27.00 🛏£23.00 🛏1
🛏1 🛏1 V 🚭 🛗 🚭
ETB 👑👑 **CO**

Arden Lodge

Mrs Lorna Price
Arden Lodge
34 Sunderland Avenue
OXFORD OX2 8DX
☎ 01865 552076

all year 🛏£30.00 🛏£22.50 🛏1
🛏1 🛏1 V 🚫 ♯♯
ETB **LI CO**

Ascot House

Miss Hall
Ascot House
283 Iffley Road
OXFORD OX4 4AQ
☎ 01865 240259
Fax 01865 727669
Email llambertti@classic.msn.com

all year 🛏£35.00 🛏£24.00 🛏1
🛏1 🛏1 🛏1 V 🔥 🚫 ♯♯ 🚭 **DRY**
AA **QQQ** RAC **HA**

Oxford Moat House

Mr Michael North
Oxford Moat House
Wolvercote Roundabout
Wolvercote
OXFORD OX2 8AL
☎ 01865 489988
Fax 01865 310259

all year 🛏£37.00 🛏£25.00 🛏69
🛏67 🛏18 V 🔥 🚫 🖵 ♯♯
ETB ♔♔♔♔♔

Pine Castle Hotel

Mrs Marilyn Morris
Pine Castle Hotel
290/292 Iffley Road
OXFORD OX4 4AE
☎ 01865 241497
Fax 01865 727230

all year 🛏£50.00 🛏£27.50 🛏6
🛏2 V 🚫 ♯♯ 🚫
ETB ♔♔ HC AA **QQQQ**

River Hotel

Mrs P Jones
River Hotel
17 Botley Road
OXFORD OX2 0AA
☎ 01865 243475
Fax 01865 724306

closed Xmas, New Year 🛏️£55.00
🛏️£37.50 🛏️6 🛏️8 🛏️2 🛏️5 **V** 🌑
🚻 **DRY** ETB 👑👑👑

The Old Parsonage Hotel

Mr Ian Hamilton
The Old Parsonage Hotel
1 Banbury Road
OXFORD OX2 6NN
☎ 01865 310210
Fax 01865 311262
Email oldparsonage@dial.pipex.com

closed Xmas 🛏️£125.00 🛏️£72.50
🛏️20 🛏️6 🛏️4 **V** 🏔️🌑 🚻

Oxford Backpackers Hostel

Dale Smith
Oxford Backpackers Hostel
9a Hythe Bridge Street
OXFORD OX1 2EW
☎ 01865 721761
Fax 01865 721761

all year Dormitory accommodation
£12.00 per person 🛏 £17.00 🛏 1
🛏 1 🚻 DRY ETB **AP**

Oxford Youth Hostel

The Manager
Oxford Youth Hostel
32 Jack Straw's Lane
OXFORD OX3 0DW
☎ 01865 762997
Fax 01865 769402

all year 🛏 £13.25 🌀

Oxford Camping International

The Proprietor
Oxford Camping International
426 Abingdon Road
OXFORD OX1 4XN
☎ 01865 246551

all year 🚐 £8.95 ⛺ £8.95 🚐 99
⛺ 30 🚽 🚿 🚰 🚻 🛒 🔌 ♿
ETB ✓✓✓✓

Salters Bros Caravan Site

The Proprietor
Salters Bros Caravan Site
Slipway Meadow Lane
Donnington Bridge
OXFORD
☎ 01865 243421

Apr - Oct 🚐 £5.00 ⛺ £5.00 🚐 12
⛺ 12 🚽 🚿 🚰 🚻 🔌

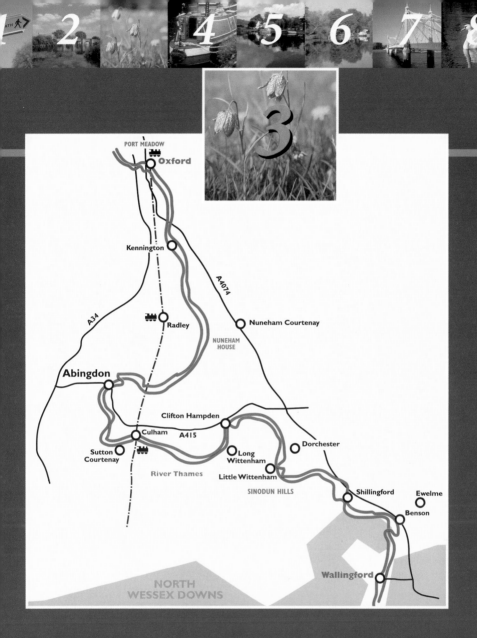

3 Oxford to Wallingford

Still essentially rural, this 38 km of the Thames Path is enhanced by the elegant city of Oxford and towns of Abingdon and Wallingford. As well as providing cultural diversions and refreshments, these are easy access points to the Path for those travelling by public transport.

3 A Taster

This section displays a variety of land use starting with the common land of Port Meadow in the northwest of Oxford, past the landscaped gardens of Nuneham House and onto views of the Sinodun Hills close to Dorchester with their distinctive clumps of trees and ancient Iron Age fort. Along with these you'll encounter modern farming of livestock and crops, the latter adding different colours to the landscape through the seasons, historic towns, attractive villages, and a marina at Benson a short distance before you reach Wallingford.

One of the best ways to arrive in Oxford is via the Thames Path from the north. If you decide not to explore this lovely city (although you are recommended to do so!) but to continue along the Path, you'll be amazed at the extent of green meadows and lack of urban intrusion. When you leave Oxford behind, with its historic buildings of Cotswold stone, you move into the clay belt where you'll find houses are mostly of brick construction.

This section includes seven locks owned and managed by the Environment Agency, all with tidy, colourful gardens and friendly lock keepers.

Landranger Maps	Explorer Maps	Pathfinder Maps
164 Oxford 175 Reading & Winsor	170 Abingdon, Wantage and Vale of White Horse	1116 (SP40/50) Oxford 1136 (SU49/59) Abingdon 1137 (SU69/79) Watlington and Stokenchurch 1156 (SU68/78) Henley & Wallingford

Public Transport Information

- National Rail - 24 hours a day   0345 484950
- Oxfordshire County Council   01865 810405

Police

Oxfordshire   01865 846000

Hospitals

Oxford   01865 741166
John Radcliffe Hospital, Headley Way, Headington, Oxford
Wallingford   01491 835533
Wallingford Community Hospital, Reading Way, Wallingford

TOURIST INFORMATION CENTRES

Oxford	The Old School, Gloucester Green, Oxford OX1 2DA. Tel 01865 726871, fax 01865 240261
Opening hours	Summer: (Easter-Sep 30) Mon-Sat 9:30-17:00, Sun 10:00-15:30. Winter: (Oct 1-Easter) Mon-Sat 9:30 17:00. Bank Holidays 10:00-15:30
Abingdon	25 Bridge Street, Abingdon OX14 3HN. Tel 01235 522711, fax 01235 535245
Opening hours	Summer: (Apr 1-Oct 31) Mon-Sat 10:00-17:00, Sun 13:30-16:15 Winter: (Nov 1-31 Mar) Mon-Fri 10:00-16:00, Sat 9:30-14:30
Wallingford	Town Hall, Market Place, Wallingford OX10 0EG. Tel 01491 826972, fax 01491 825844
Opening hours	All year: Mon-Sat 10:00-16:00

KENNINGTON

 SP5202 🥾 0.5km

🚂 Oxford 5.7km 🚲 Tandem ✕
Scholar Gypsy, Westwood Country
Hotel ✕ ✉ 🛍 |||||||||||| ☎
S M T W T F S

The Lawns

Mr & Mrs A Marshall
The Lawns
10 Jackson Drive
Kennington
OXFORD OX1 5LL
☎ 01865 739595

all year 🛏£20.00 🛏£20.00 🛏2
🛏2 V 🚭 🚻 over 10 yrs **DRY** 🚗
ETB 👑 CO

NUNEHAM COURTENAY

SU5599 🥾 3.5km **Cross river at
Sandford Lock or Clifton Hampden**

🚂 Oxford 10.5km ✉
🛍 |||||||||||| ☎
S M T W T F S

The Old Bakery

Mrs M Howard
The Old Bakery
Nuneham Courtenay
OXFORD OX44 9NX
☎ 01865 343585
Fax 01865 343585

all year 🛏£25.00 🛏£25.00 🛏1
🛏4 🛏4 🛏2 V 🚭🚭 **not Sun** 🐕
🚻 🚭 ♿ **DRY** 🚗 🚽 ETB 👑👑 HC

ABINGDON

SU4997 On the Path **Town** with full range of services

Radley 3.5km

Rowen Guest House

Mr & Mrs R Woodford
Rowen Guest House
42a Oxford Road
ABINGDON OX14 2DZ
01235 522066

all year £24.00 £17.50 1
1 3 1 V ✚ ✝✝

The Old Vicarage

Mrs McLellan
The Old Vicarage
17 Park Crescent
ABINGDON OX14 1DF
01235 522561

all year £24.00 £22.00 1
1 1 V ✚ ✝✝ ⊘ **DRY**

Mrs Susie Howard

22 East St Helen Street
ABINGDON OX14 5EB
01235 550979
Fax 01235 533278

all year £25.00 £22.00 1
1 1 V ⚠ ✚ ✝✝ ⊘ **DRY**

Brewer's Cottage

Mrs J Hayman
Brewer's Cottage
3 Brewer's Court
Winsmore Lane
ABINGDON OX14 5BG
01235 522324

all year £25.00 £22.50 1 V
✚ ✝✝ ⊘

Abingdon Four Pillars

Ms Sue Randall
Abingdon Four Pillars
Marcham Road
ABINGDON OX14 1TZ
01235 553456
Fax 01235 554117
Email enquiries@four-pillars.co.uk

all year £48.00 £28.00 10
17 21 7 V ⚠ ✚ 🖃 ✝✝ ♿
ETB 👑👑👑👑 CO

Conifers

Mrs M Bird
Conifers
5 Galley Field
Radley Road
ABINGDON OX14 3RU
☎ 01235 521088

Mar - Oct £22.00 £17.00 3
not Sun DRY

Pastures Green

Mrs M White
Pastures Green
46 Picklers Hill
ABINGDON OX14 2BB
☎ 01235 521369
Fax spencer.white@btinternet.com

all year £17.00 £16.00 1
1 1 V DRY

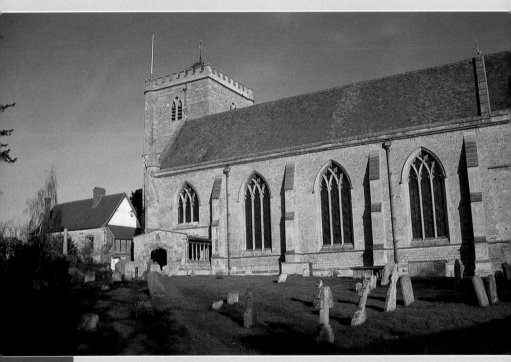

CULHAM

SU5095 ⌂ On the Path
🚂 Culham 2.5km 🍺 Railway Inn ✕
Waggon & Horses ✕ Lion ✕ 📞

The Railway Inn

Mr S M Wilson
The Railway Inn
The Station Approach
Culham Station
ABINGDON OX14 3BT
☎ 01235 528046
Fax 01235 525183

all year 🛏 £35.00 🛏 £25.00 🛏 2
🛏 4 🛏 1 V 🔥 🚭 not Sun 🔌 👶 🚭
♿ DRY 🚗 🏠 ETB ♛♛♛

🚐 £15.00 ⛺ £5.00 🚐 5 ⛺ 10 🔥
👶 🔥 🚭 not Sun 🚗 🏠

SUTTON COURTENAY

SU5093 ⌂ 1.5km **Cross river at
Culham Bridge** 🚂 Didcot 5.5km
🍺 several ✕ ✉ 🏤 |||||||||||
S M T W T F S
📞

Bekynton House

Ms Sue Cornwall
Bekynton House
7 The Green
Sutton Courtenay
ABINGDON OX14 4AE
☎ 01235 848888
Fax 01235 848436

all year 🛏 £25.00 🛏 £25.00 🛏 1
🛏 1 🛏 1 V 🔥 🚭 👶 🚭 DRY 🏠

The Fish

Mr & Mrs M Gaffney
The Fish
4 Appleford Road
Sutton Courtenay
ABINGDON OX14 4NQ
☎ 01235 848242
Fax 01235 848014

all year 🛏 £35.00 🛏 £22.50 🛏 2 V
🚭 DRY 🏠 🚗

CLIFTON HAMPDEN

SU5495 On the Path
Culham 1.8km Plough Inn
Barley Mow

The Plough Inn Restaurant & Hotel

Mr Yuksel Bektas
The Plough Inn Restaurant & Hotel
Abingdon Road
Clifton Hampden
ABINGDON OX14 3EG
01865 407811
Fax 01865 407136

all year £62.50 £41.25 9
2 V DRY

Bridge House Caravan Site

Miss E Gower
Bridge House Caravan Site
Bridge House
Clifton Hampden
ABINGDON OX14 3EH
01865 407725

Apr – Oct £8.00 £5.00 40
12 DRY

LONG WITTENHAM

SU5493 2.5km **Cross river at Days Lock or Clifton Hampden**
Culham 3.8km several

Witta's Ham Cottage

Mrs Jill Mellor
Witta's Ham Cottage
High Street
Long Wittenham
ABINGDON OX14 4QH
01865 407686
Fax 01865 407469

closed Xmas £24.00 £21.00 1
1 1 V over 2 yrs
DRY

LITTLE WITTENHAM

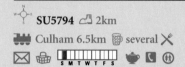

SU5693 0.5km
Culham 5.5km

Rooks Orchard

Mrs Deborah Welfare
Rooks Orchard
Little Wittenham
ABINGDON OX14 4QY
☎ 01865 407765
Fax 01865 407765
Email jonathan.welfare@which.net

closed Xmas £28.00 £24.00
1 1 V not Sun over
8 yrs DRY ETB HC

Day's Lock

The Lock Keeper
Day's Lock
DORCHESTER ON THAMES
☎ 01865 407768

Easter-Sep 5
Available only to walkers and boaters.

DORCHESTER

SU5794 2km
Culham 6.5km several
S M T W T F S

The George Hotel

Mr Michael Pinder
The George Hotel
25 High Street
DORCHESTER ON THAMES
OX10 7HH
☎ 01865 340404
Fax 01865 341620

all year £62.50 £40.00 3
9 5 1 V
DRY AA ★★★ DL RAC ★★★

White Hart Hotel

Mr Joe Barrow
White Hart Hotel
High Street
DORCHESTER ON THAMES
OX10 7HN
☎ 01865 340074
Fax 01865 341082

all year £65.00 £37.50 2
7 6 4 V
DRY AA ★★ RAC ★★★

SHILLINGFORD

SU5992 ⌂ On the Path

🚂 Cholsey 8.3km 🍴 Kingfisher ✗

Shillingford Bridge Hotel ✗ 📞

Marsh House

Mrs Patricia Nickson
Marsh House
Court Drive
Shillingford
WALLINGFORD OX10 7ER
☎ 01865 858496
Fax 01865 858496

all year 🛏£25.00 🛏£20.00 🛏2 🛏1
V 🔥 🚫 ⚥ over 8 yrs 🚭 DRY 🍴

North Farm

Mrs Hilary Warburton
North Farm
Shillingford Hill
WALLINGFORD OX10 8NB
☎ 01865 858406
Fax 01865 858519

closed Xmas, New Year 🛏£28.00
🛏£24.00 🛏1 🛏1 V 🔥 🚫 ⚥
over 10 yrs 🚭 DRY 🚗 🍴
ETB 👑👑 HC

BENSON

SU6191 ⌂ On the Path

🚂 Cholsey 8.2km 🍴 several ✗ ✉

🧺 |||||||| 🫖 📞 ♿
    S M T W T F S

Hale Farm

Mrs A Belcher
Hale Farm
Hale Road
Benson
WALLINGFORD OX10 6NE
☎ 01491 836818

Easter-Oct 🛏£15.00 🛏£15.00 🛏1
🛏1 🛏1 V 🔥 🚫 ⚥ 🚭 DRY
🚗 🍴

Benson Cruiser Station

Mr Adrian Tilbury
Benson Cruiser Station
Benson
WALLINGFORD OX10 6SJ
☎ 01491 838304

Apr-Oct 🚐£8.00 ⛺£4.00 🚐25
⛺25 🗄 🚿 🚽 ♿ 🧴 🛍 🔥 🚫
🍳 ♿ DRY

EWELME

SU6491 3.5km

Cholsey 10km

Shepherd's Hut

Dormer Cottage

Mrs J Standbridge
Dormer Cottage
High Street
Ewelme
WALLINGFORD OX10 6HQ
01491 833987

closed Xmas £18.00 £17.00 1
1 V not Sun over 10 yrs DRY

WALLINGFORD

SU6089 On the Path **Town**
with full range of services

Cholsey 4.7km

Mrs E J Bernard

52 Blackstone Road
WALLINGFORD OX10 8JL
01491 839339

all year £15.00 £15.00 1
1 DRY

The Studio

Mrs Pamela Smith
The Studio
85 Wantage Road
WALLINGFORD OX10 0LT
01491 837277
Fax 01491 825036

all year £20.00 £20.00 2
1 1 over 4 yrs
DRY

The Dolphin

Mrs K Walker
The Dolphin
2 St Mary's Street
WALLINGFORD OX10 0EL
☎ 01491 837377

all year 🛏£20.00 🛏£20.00 🛏1 🛏3
V 🌙 🚭

Munts Mill

Mrs Mary Broster
Munts Mill
Castle Lane
WALLINGFORD OX10 0BN
☎ 01491 836654

all year 🛏£20.00 🛏2 🌙 🚭 DRY

The Nook

Mrs C Colclough
The Nook
2 Thames Street
WALLINGFORD OX10 0BK
☎ 01491 834214

all year 🛏£35.00 🛏£22.50 🛏1
🛏1 🛏1 V 🔥 🌙 👫

The George Hotel

Mr Peter Voss
The George Hotel
High Street
WALLINGFORD OX10 0BS
☎ 01491 836665
Fax 01491 825359

all year 🛏£49.00 🛏£48.00 🛏14
🛏16 🛏8 🛏1 V 🔥 🌙 👫 ♿
DRY 🍴 AA ★★★ RAC ★★★

Section Four

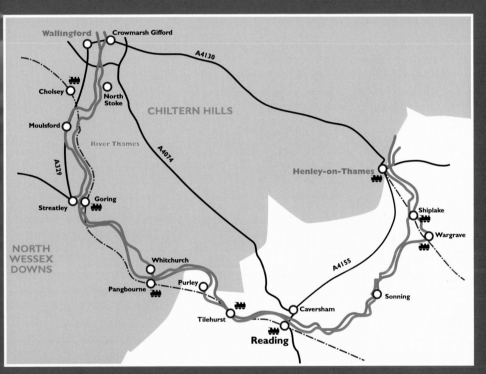

4 Wallingford to Henley on Thames

A 44 km stretch of the Path alongside the Thames during an especially serene stage as it enters the Chiltern Hills which provide a wonderful wooded backdrop. You'll regularly find settlements ranging in size from villages to the large town of Reading many of which provide good public transport access to the Path and refreshments.

4 A Taster

The first few kilometres of your walk from Wallingford pass through very open countryside with large undulating arable fields stretching away to the east to a beech wood skyline. Soon, however, you reach the Goring Gap with the Berkshire Downs rising on one side and the Chiltern Hills on the other. This is the narrowest part of the Thames Valley and the hills to either side seem almost like mountains compared to the flatness of the Oxfordshire clay vale through which the river has recently flowed.

At the twin settlements of Streatley and Goring the Thames Path is crossed by another of England's 13 National Trails, The Ridgeway. This ancient route enters the Goring Gap from the chalk downs to the west and then heads northeast along the Chilterns escarpment having followed the Thames for a few kilometres on the opposite bank to the Thames Path.

Between Goring and Mapledurham the Path, its river, the railway and main road all squeeze together between chalk hills clad with the trees which give the Chiltern Hills its character. Your approach to Reading through Purley is currently a temporary one whilst a hopefully less urban route can be found, but the Path through Reading itself is surprisingly pleasant for it passes through the least urbanised area.

From Reading to Sonning cyclists can share the Path, but from Sonning, with its lovely 18th century hump-backed bridge, the Path narrows and is for walkers only. As you walk towards Henley, famous for its Royal Regatta, you'll enjoy a landscape of gentle wooded hills, fine houses, and, of course, the ever widening Thames.

There are a few places where the route of the Path is still temporary whilst the lengthy legal work to create new footpaths is completed. These are at Moulsford, Purley and Shiplake. However, it is hoped that this work will be finished soon.

Landranger Maps	Explorer Maps	Pathfinder Maps
175 Reading & Windsor	170 Abingdon, Wantage and Vale of White Horse	1156 (SU68/67) Henley & Wallingford
174 Newbury & Wantage	171 Chiltern Hills West (due Spring 1999)	1155 (SP48/58) Wantage & Didcot
		1171 (SU47/57) Hermitage & Chieveley
		1172 (SU67/77) Reading

Public Transport Information
- National Rail - 24 hours a day   0345 484950
- Oxfordshire County Council   01865 810405

Police
Oxfordshire & Berkshire   01865 846000

Hospitals
Wallingford 01491 835533
Wallingford Community Hospital, Reading Way, Wallingford
Reading 0118 9875111
The Royal Berkshire Hospital, London Road, Reading
Henley 01491 572544
Townlands Hospital, York Rd, Henley

TOURIST INFORMATION CENTRES

Wallingford   Town Hall, Market Place, Wallingford OX10 0EG.
                    Tel 01491 826972, fax 01491 825844
Opening hours   All year: Mon-Sat 10:00-16:00

Reading   Town Hall, Blagrave Street, Reading RG1 1QH. Tel
                    0118 956 6226, fax 0118 939 9885
Opening hours   All year: Mon-Fri 10:00-17:00, Sat 10:00-16:00

Henley-on-Thames   Town Hall, Market Place, Henley-on-Thames
                    RG9 2AQ. Tel 01491 578034, fax 01491 411766
Opening hours   Summer: (Mar 31-Sep 30) daily 10:00-19:00
                    Winter: (Oct 1-Mar 31) daily 10:00-16:00

CROWMARSH GIFFORD

SU6189 0.5km **Cross river at Wallingford Bridge**

Cholsey 5.7km

Queen's Head ✕ Bell ✕ ✉

S M T W T F S

Little Gables

Mrs A Reeves
Little Gables
166 Crowmarsh Hill
Crowmarsh Gifford
WALLINGFORD OX10 8BG
☎ 01491 837834
Fax 01491 837834

all year £30.00 £25.00 1
1 1 V ♦ ⊘ ✤ ⊘ **DRY**
🚗 ⊟ ETB ♛♛ CO

Riverside Park & Pool

Mr Graham Kearney
Riverside Park & Pool
The Street
Wallingford Bridge
WALLINGFORD OX10 8EB
☎ 01491 835232
Fax 01491 835232

May-Sep 28 28 ▥ ⊘ ⊘ ♿

Bridge Villa Camping & Caravan Park

Mr E L Townsend
Bridge Villa Camping & Caravan Park
Crowmarsh Gifford
WALLINGFORD OX10 8HB
☎ 01491 836860
Fax 01491 839103

Feb-Dec £6.00 £4.00 111
111 ▥ ⊘ ⊘ ⊘ ⊘ ⊘

NORTH STOKE

✧ SU6086 🛏 2.7km **Cross river at A4130 bridge south of Wallingford or Goring** 🚂 Goring & Streatley 6.6km ☎

The Springs Hotel & Golf Club

Miss Andrea Wolf
The Springs Hotel & Golf Club
Wallingford Road
North Stoke
WALLINGFORD OX10 6BE
☎ 01491 836687
Fax 01491 836877
Email springsuk@aol.com

all year 🛏 £89.00 🛏 £61.50 🛏 23
🛏 3 🛏 4 **V** 🅰 🚭 🛊 ♿ DRV 🎁
AA ★★★ RAC ★★★

MOULSFORD

✧ SU5983 🛏 On the Path 🚂 Cholsey 3.4km 🍺 Beetle & Wedge ✕ ☎

White House

Mrs Maria Watsham
White House
Moulsford
WALLINGFORD OX10 9JD
☎ 01491 651397

closed Xmas, New Year 🛏 £25.00
🛏 £22.50 🛏 1 🛏 1 🛏 1 **V** 🅰 🚭
🛊 🚭 DRV ETB 👑 HC

The Beetle and Wedge Hotel

Mrs Kate Smith
The Beetle and Wedge Hotel
Ferry Lane
Moulsford
WALLINGFORD OX10 9JF
☎ 01491 651381
Fax 01491 651376

all year 🛏 £90.00 🛏 £67.50 🛏 10 **V**
🅰 🚭 🛏 🛊 ♿ DRV 🚗

STREATLEY

⊕ **SU5980** ⌂ On the Path

🚂 Goring & Streatley 1.2km

🍺 Swan Diplomat Hotel ✕ Bull ✕ 📞

The Swan Diplomat

Miss Vanessa Lane
The Swan Diplomat
Streatley
READING RG8 9HR
☎ 01491 873737
Fax 01491 872554
Email sales@swan-diplomat.co.uk

all year 🛏£68.50 🛏£52.50 🛏9
🛏27 🛏10 V 🔥 🚫 ▣ 🛉 ♿
RAC ★★★★ AA ★★★★
ETB 👑👑👑👑 HC

Streatley on Thames Youth Hostel

The Manager
Streatley on Thames Youth Hostel
Hill House
Reading Road
Streatley
READING RG8 9JJ
☎ 01491 872278
Fax 01491 873056

all year 🛏£13.25 🔥 🚫

GORING

⊕ **SU6081** ⌂ On the Path

🚂 Goring & Streatley 🍺 several ✕

✉ 🧺 ▦ S M T W T F S 🍵

£ Midlands 📷 Lloyds 📞 ♿

Leyland Guest House

Mrs Betty Wiltshire
Leyland Guest House
3 Wallingford Road
GORING RG8 0AX
☎ 01491 872119

Easter-Oct 🛏£20.00 🛏£18.50 🛏1
🛏1 🛏1 V 🔥 🚫 ▣ 🛉 DRY

The Queens Arms

Mrs B Carter
The Queens Arms
Reading Road
GORING RG8 0ER
☎ 01491 872825
Fax 01491 872825

all year 🛏£20.00 🛏£20.00 🛏2
🛏1 🔥 🚫 ▣ 🛉 DRY 🎁

The John Barleycorn

Mr Anthony Fincham
The John Barleycorn
Manor Road
GORING RG8 9DP
☎ 01491 872509

all year 🛏 £23.00 🛏 £19.50 🛏 1
🛏 2 🛏 1 🛏 1 V ⚠ 🚫 🖼 ✨ DRY
ETB 👑

Mrs Norma Ewen

14 Mountfield
Wallingford Road
GORING RG8 0BE
☎ 01491 872029

all year 🛏 £23.00 🛏 £20.00 🛏 1
🛏 1 🛏 1 🛏 1 🚫 ✨ ♿ DRY 🎁

942   2556

9780961032a

Miller of Mansfield

Mr Martin Williamson
Miller of Mansfield
High Street
GORING RG8 9AW
☎ 01491 872829
Fax 01491 874200

all year 🛏£47.50 🛏£32.50 🛏 5
🛏4 🛏1 V 🚳 🚫 ⛔ ⅋⅋ DRY
ETB 👑👑👑 CO

WHITCHURCH-ON-THAMES

🧭 **SU6377** ⛺ On the Path
🚂 Pangbourne 1km
🍺 Ferry Boat ✖ Greyhound ✖ 📞

The Rectory

Mrs Ann Hughes
The Rectory
High Street
Whitchurch-on-Thames
READING RG8 7DF
☎ 0118 984 3219
Fax 0118 984 5976
Email rmillree@aol.com

all year 🛏£25.00 🛏£25.00 🛏1
🛏2 V 🚳 🚫 ⅋⅋ 🚭 DRY 📦

PANGBOURNE

🧭 **SU6376** ⛺ On the Path
🚂 Pangbourne 🏨 several ✖ ✉
🧺 | S M T W T F S | ☕ £ National
Westminster, Lloyds 🅿 📞 ⅋⅋ ⛺

Weir View House

Mrs Avril Cooper
Weir View House
9 Shooters Hill
PANGBOURNE RG8 7DZ
☎ 0118 984 2120
Fax 0118 984 2120

all year 🛏£28.00 🛏£22.50 🛏1
🛏1 🛏2 V 🚫 ⅋⅋ 🚭 ETB 👑👑

The Copper Inn Hotel & Restaurant

Mr Michel Rosso
The Copper Inn Hotel & Restaurant
Church Road
PANGBOURNE RG8 7AR
☎ 0118 984 2244
Fax 0118 984 5542

all year 🛏£45.00 🛏£45.00 🛏3
🛏14 🛏4 🛏1 V 🚳 🚫 ⛔ ⅋⅋ ♿
AA ★★★ RAC ★★★ ETB HC

01189
427517

The Tithe Barn

Mrs Francesca Wakefield
The Tithe Barn
Tidmarsh
PANGBOURNE RG8 8ER
☎ 0118 984 2829

closed Xmas 🛏️£65.00 🛏️£32.50
🛏️1 🚭 🚫 🚗 self-contained
apartment

TILEHURST

⊕ **SU6674** 🛏️ On the Path
🚆 Tilehurst 🏨 Calcot Hotel ✗
Murdoch's ✗ ✉️ 🧺 |‖‖‖‖‖‖‖‖‖|
S M T W T F S
🫖 £ Lloyds National
Westminster Barclays 📞 ♿

Beethoven's Hotel

Miss P L Dagnall
Beethoven's Hotel
Oxford Road
Tilehurst
READING RG31 6TG
☎ 0118 942 7517
Fax 0118 941 7629

all year 🛏️£25.00 🛏️£17.50 🛏️5
🛏️3 🛏️3 **V** 🅿️ 🚭 not Sun 🍴 🍼 🚲
ETB 👑👑👑👑 **AP**

Warren Dene Hotel

Mrs M L Jardine
Warren Dene Hotel
1017 Oxford Road
Tilehurst
READING RG31 6TL
☎ 0118 942 2556
Fax 0118 945 1096
Email wdh@globalnet.co.uk

all year 🛏️£26.00 🛏️£19.00 🛏️1
🛏️2 🛏️2 🛏️3 🚭 🍼 **DRY**
ETB 👑👑👑👑 **CO**

READING

⊕ **SU7173** 🛏️ On the Path **Large
town with full range of services**
🚆 Reading ℹ️

Berkeley Guest House

Mr & Mrs G Hubbard
Berkeley Guest House
32 Berkeley Avenue
READING RG1 6JE
☎ 0118 959 5699

all year 🛏️£20.00 🛏️£19.00 🛏️1
🛏️1 🛏️1 🛏️1 **V** 🅿️ 🚭 📺 🍼 **DRY**
ETB **LI**

The George Hotel

Mr John Hamilton-Duirs
The George Hotel
10-12 King Street
READING RG1 2HE
☎ 0118 957 3445
Fax 0118 950 8614

all year 🛏️£22.50 🛏️£22.50 🛏️18
🛏️14 🛏️30 🛏️2 V ◐ ♀♂ DRY 🗲
AA ★★

Dittisham Guest House

Mr Frank Harding
Dittisham Guest House
63 Tilehurst Road
READING RG30 2JL
☎ 0118 956 9483
Fax 0118 956 9483

all year 🛏️£23.00 🛏️£17.50 🛏️2
🛏️1 🛏️1 V ◐ ♀♂ DRY ETB LI CO

Thames House Hotel

Mrs Breakspear
Thames House Hotel
18-19 Thames Side
READING RG1 8DR
☎ 0118 950 7951
Fax 0118 950 7951

closed Xmas, New Year 🛏£27.50
🛏£22.50 🛏4 🛏2 🛏2 🛏2 🖊
🚫 🛉

Rainbow Corner Hotel

Mr D Staples
Rainbow Corner Hotel
132-138 Caversham Road
READING RG1 8AY
☎ 0118 958 8140
Fax 0118 958 6500
Email rchhotel@aol.com

all year 🛏£35.95 🛏£22.95 🛏9
🛏15 🛏7 🛏1 V 🖊🚫 not Sun
🛉 ♿ **DRY** ETB 👑👑👑👑 CO
AA ★★ RAC ★★

Abbey House Hotel

Mr & Mrs Peck
Abbey House Hotel
118 Connaught Road
READING RG30 2UF
☎ 0118 959 0549
Fax 0118 956 9299
Email abbey.house@btinternet.com

closed Xmas 🛏£36.00 🛏£23.00 🛏5
🛏5 🛏8 🛏1 V 🖊🚫 🛉 **DRY** 🚗
ETB 👑👑👑 CO AA QQQQ
RAC **AC**

Quality Hotel

Mr Stuart Hall
Quality Hotel
654 Oxford Road
READING RG30 1EH
☎ 0118 950 0541
Fax 0118 956 7220

all year 🛏£80.00 🛏£47.75 🛏3
🛏68 🛏10 🛏13 V 🖊🚫 🛉
RAC ★★★ AA ★★★

Rainbow Lodge Hotel

Mr Cary
Rainbow Lodge Hotel
152 Caversham Road
READING RG1 8AY
☎ 0118 958 8140

Abadair House

Mrs Clifford
Abadair House
46 Redlands Road
READING RG1 5HE
☎ 0118 986 3792

Brackenhurst Guest House

Mrs Stocker
Brackenhurst Guest House
230 Wokingham Road
READING RG6 1JS
☎ 0118 966 7829

Bath Hotel

The Proprietor
Bath Hotel
54 Bath Road
READING RG1 6PG
☎ 0118 957 2019

Crescent Hotel

The Proprietor
Crescent Hotel
35 Coley Avenue
READING RG1 6LL
☎ 0118 950 7980

Ramada Hotel

Ms Karen Jennings
Ramada Hotel
Oxford Road
READING RG1 7RH
☎ 0118 958 6222
Fax 0118 959 7842

Comfort Inn

Mr Higgins
Comfort Inn
119 Kendrick Road
READING RG1 5EB
☎ 0118 931 1311

The Ship Hotel

The Proprietor
The Ship Hotel
4-8 Duke Street
READING RG1 4RY
0118 958 3455

CAVERSHAM

⌖ **SU7174** 🛏 **0.5km Cross river
at Caversham Bridge for full range
of services in Reading**

🚂 Reading 1.5km

Mrs Alison Prentice

90 St Peter's Avenue
Caversham
READING RG4 7DL
☎ 0118 947 1682

closed Jul, Oct, Dec 🛏 £22.00
🛏 £20.00 🛏 1 🛏 1 **V** 🚫 🚭

SHIPLAKE

⌖ **SU7678** 🛏 On the Path
🚌 Shiplake 2km
🍺 Plowden Arms ✕ Bottle & Glass ✕
Coach & Horses ✕ ✉
🛒 ▮▯▯▯▯▯▯ ☾
    S M T W T F S

The Baskerville Arms

Mr & Mrs Cannon
The Baskerville Arms
7 Station Road
Shiplake
HENLEY-ON-THAMES RG9 3NY
☎ 0118 940 3332

all year 🛏 £40.00 🛏 £25.00 🛏 1
🛏 2 🛏 1 **V** 🏍 🚫 📷 ⛹ **DRY**

Mrs Janet Fletcher

1 Kingsley
Crowsley Road
Lower Shiplake
HENLEY-ON-THAMES RG9 3LU
☎ 0118 940 3626

all year 🛏 £20.00 🛏 1 🚫 🚭 **DRY**

4 Wallingford to Henley on Thames

WARGRAVE

⊕ **SU7878** ⌂ 5km **Cross river at Sonning or Henley** 🚌 Wargrave

🏨 several ✕ ✉ 🧺 ▦▦▦▦▦▦▦
S M T W T F S

📞 ♿

Somewhere To Stay

Mr Roger Fisher
Somewhere To Stay
c/o Loddon Acres
Bath Road
Twyford
READING RG10 9RU
☎ 0118 934 5880
Fax 0118 934 5880

all year 🛏️£29.90 🛏️£22.25 🛏️1
🛏️1 🛏️1 🛏️1 V 🚫 📷 🕇 🚭 DRY
ETB ♕♕♕ HC

HENLEY-ON-THAMES

⊕ **SU7682** ⌂ On the Path **Town with full range of services**
🚌 Henley-on-Thames ℹ️

Vine Cottage

Mrs Blanche Williams
Vine Cottage
53 Northfield End
HENLEY-ON-THAMES RG9 2JJ
☎ 01491 573545
Fax 01491 410707

closed Xmas 🛏️£19.00 🛏️£19.00 🛏️2
🛏️1 🚫 🕇 over 10 yrs 🚭

Ledard

Mrs Irene Howard
Ledard
Rotherfield Road
HENLEY-ON-THAMES RG9 1NN
☎ 01491 575611

all year 🛏️£20.00 🛏️£18.00 🛏️1
🛏️1 🛏️1 V 🔥 🚫 🕇 🚭 DRY 🚗 🎁

Coldharbour House

Mrs Diana Jones
Coldharbour House
3 Coldharbour Close
HENLEY-ON-THAMES RG9 1QF
☎ 01491 575229
Fax 01491 575229
Email
coldharbourhouse@compuserve.com

closed Xmas 🛏️ £22.00 🛏️ £20.00 🛏️ 1
🛏️ 1 🛏️ 1 V 🚫 📶 🕴 🚭 **DRY** 🚐
ETB **LI CO**

Mrs Cynthia Watson

72 Reading Road
HENLEY-ON-THAMES RG9 1AU
☎ 01491 574081
Fax 070707 18863

all year 🛏️ £22.00 🛏️ £20.00 🛏️ 2
🛏️ 1 🛏️ 1 🛏️ 1 V 🔥 🚫 📶 🕴 🚭
DRY 🎁

Avalon

Mrs Pauline Willis
Avalon
36 Queen Street
HENLEY-ON-THAMES RG9 1AP
☎ 01491 577829

all year 🛏️ £22.00 🛏️ £20.00 🛏️ 1
🛏️ 2 🛏️ 1 🚫 🕴 over 10 yrs 🚭 ♿
ETB **CO**

Lenwade

Mrs Jacquie Williams
Lenwade
3 Western Road
HENLEY-ON-THAMES RG9 1JL
☎ 01491 573468
Fax 01491 573468
Email lenwadeuk@compuserve.com

all year 🛏️ £25.00 🛏️ £25.00 🛏️ 2
🛏️ 1 V 🔥 🚫 🕴 🚭 **DRY**
ETB 👑 👑 **HC** AA **QQQQQ**

Old Bell House

Mrs Duckett
Old Bell House
Northfield End
HENLEY-ON-THAMES RG9 2JG
☎ 01491 574350
Fax 01491 571544
Email antonyduckett
@antonydesign.demon.uk

all year 🛏£25.00 🛏£25.00 🛏1
🛏1 ♨🚭🕭🏠🚻🚭 DRY 🏮

Abbotts Leigh

Mrs K Bridlekirk
Abbotts Leigh
107 St Marks Road
HENLEY-ON-THAMES RG9 1LP
☎ 01491 572982

all year 🛏£26.50 🛏£22.50 🛏1
🛏1 🛏1 V 🚭 DRY 🚗 🏮

Alftrudis

Mrs Sue Lambert
Alftrudis
8 Norman Avenue
HENLEY-ON-THAMES RG9 1SG
☎ 01491 573099
Fax 01491 411747

all year 🛏£35.00 🛏£22.50 🛏2
🛏1 V 🚭 🚻 over 8 yrs 🚭
ETB 👑 HC

The Red Lion Hotel

Mr James Shawcross
The Red Lion Hotel
Hart Street
HENLEY ON THAMES RG9 2AR
☎ 01491 572161
Fax 01491 410039

all year 🛏£93.00 🛏£66.00 🛏3
🛏12 🛏10 🛏1 V ♨🚭🚻 DRY 🏮
AA ★★★

Swiss Farm International Camping

The Proprietor
Swiss Farm International Camping
Marlow Road
HENLEY-ON-THAMES RG9 2HY
☎ 01491 573419

Mar-Oct

Henley on Thames to Windsor

Section Five

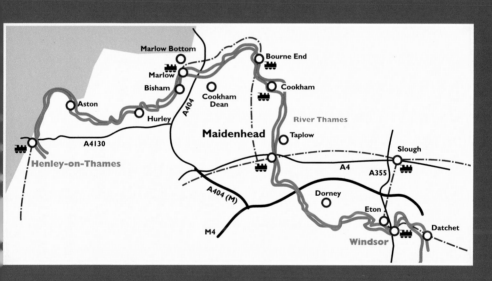

5 Henley on Thames to Windsor

The pleasures of this 37 km stretch of the Path lie in the combination of walking beside the now mature river surrounded by the wooded slopes of the Chiltern Hills and the opportunity of exploring numerous pretty villages and towns, all with historical associations with famous people. And, of course, this section is very easily reached by public transport.

L eaving Henley you follow the whole length of the Royal Regatta course through
increasingly rural grass meadows to Temple Island the starting point for the
races. The small temple is in fact a fishing lodge built as a landscape feature to
enhance the view from nearby Fawley Court. Indeed, along the whole route to
Windsor you'll come across many fine houses with landscaped gardens or parks,
now owned, one imagines, by the rich and famous of today.

Before you reach the attractive town of Marlow the Path does usually become busier.
You'll also have passed Hurley and Bisham, both with tremendous stories from the
past and fine buildings to see. Marlow, like Henley, has its own regatta and brewery
(Wethereds) and is arguably set in the most beautiful stretch of the Thames Valley.

Onto Cookham and beyond to a reach of the river set between towering trees,
magnificent during autumn, above which you'll catch a glimpse of Cliveden House.
This gained a colourful reputation for political intrigue both in the 1930s and later
in the 1960s when the Profumo affair hit the headlines as a result of 'activities' in
one of the riverside cottages you'll see on the far bank.

Maidenhead is prettily suburban having developed during the Edwardian era when
the river here, and town, was packed with day trippers from London. From here the
river becomes more commercial, the population pressure increases and the banks
become lined with houses, many of them grand. Views of Windsor Castle are visible
for many miles high on the last chalky outcrop of the Chilterns.

Landranger Maps	Explorer Maps	Pathfinder Maps
175 Reading & Windsor	171 Chiltern Hills West (due Spring 1999) 172 Chiltern Hills East (due Spring 1999) 160 Windsor, Weybridge and Bracknell	1156 (SU68/67) Henley & Wallingford 1157 (SP88/98) Maidenhead & Marlow 1173 (SU87/97) Windsor

5 *A Taster*

Public Transport Information
- National Rail - 24 hours a day   0345 484950
- Oxfordshire County Council   01865 810405
- Buckinghamshire County Council 0345 382000

Police
Berkshire & Buckinghamshire   01865 846000

Hospitals
Henley 01491 572544
Townlands Hospital, York Road, Henley
High Wycombe 01494 526161
Wycombe General Hospital, Queen Alexandra Road, High Wycombe

TOURIST INFORMATION CENTRES

Henley-on-Thames	Town Hall, Market Place, Henley-on-Thames RG9 2AQ. Tel 01491 578034, fax 01491 411766
Opening hours	Summer: (Mar 31-Sep 30) daily 10:00-19:00 Winter: (Oct 1-Mar 31) daily 10:00-16:00
Marlow	31 High Street, Marlow SL7 1AU. Tel 01628 483597, fax 01628 471915
Opening hours	Summer: (Easter-Sep 30) Mon-Fri 9:00-17:00, Sat 9:30-16:30, Sun 10:00-16:30 Winter: (Oct 1-Easter) Mon-Fri 9:00-17:00, Sat 9:30-16:30
Maidenhead	The Library, St Ives Road, Maidenhead SL6 1QU. Tel/fax 01628 781110
Opening hours	All year: Mon, Tue, Thu, Fri 9:30-17:00, Sat 9:30-16:00
Windsor	24 High Street, Windsor SL4 1LH. Tel 01753 743900 (general information) 01753 743907 (accommodation bookings), fax 01753 743904.
Opening hours	Mon-Sun 10:00-17:00 (subject to seasonal changes)

ASTON

↗ **SU7884** ⌂ 0.5km 🚂 Henley-on-Thames 4.5km 🍴 Flower Pot ✕ closed Sun pm 📞

The Flower Pot

Ms Pat Thatcher
The Flower Pot
Aston
HENLEY-ON-THAMES RG9 3DG
☎ 01491 574721

all year 🛏 £39.00 🛏 £24.50 🛏 2 🛏 1 V 🚫 not Sun ♿ &

HURLEY

↗ **SU8283** ⌂ On the Path 🚂 Marlow 6km 🍴 several ✕ ✉ 🧺 |‖‖‖‖‖‖‖| S M T W T F S 📞

Ye Olde Bell Hotel

Mr Jonathan Squire
Ye Olde Bell Hotel
High Street
Hurley
MAIDENHEAD SL6 5LX
☎ 01628 825881
Fax 01628 825939

all year 🛏 £64.50 🛏 £49.50 🛏 7 🛏 33 🛏 1 🛏 3 V 🚫 🔒 ♿
ETB 👑👑👑👑👑 HC

Hurley Farm Caravan & Camping Park

Mr D R Burfitt
Hurley Farm Caravan & Camping Park
Estate Office
Hurley Farm
Hurley
MAIDENHEAD SL6 5NE
☎ 01628 823501
Fax 01628 825533

Mar-Oct 🚐 £6.00 ⛺ £5.50 🚐 140
⛺ 60 📱 🚿 🚽 ⓗ 🔲 🗄 🟢 🖼
♿ **DRY** 🚗 ETB ✓✓✓✓

Hurley Lock

The Lock Keeper
Hurley Lock
Mill Lane
Hurley
MAIDENHEAD SL6 1SA
☎ 01628 824334

Apr-Sep ⛺ 10 📱 🚿 🚽 ⓗ

MARLOW

🧭 SU8586 ⛺ On the Path Town
with full range of services
🚂 Marlow ℹ

Acha Pani B&B

Mrs Mary Cowling
Acha Pani B&B
Bovingdon Green
MARLOW SL7 2JL
☎ 01628 483435
Fax 01628 483435

all year 🛏 £17.00 🛏 £17.00 🛏 1
🛏 1 🚿 1 V 🔥 🟢 not Sun, Mon 🖼
♀♂ **DRY** 🚗 ETB **LI CO**

Mrs S R Bendall

5 Pound Lane
MARLOW SL7 2AE
☎ 01628 482649

closed Xmas, New Year 🛏 £28.00
🛏 £20.00 🛏 1 🚿 1 V 🔥 🟢 ♀♂
over 10 yrs 🚭 **DRY** ETB **LI CO**

Huxley

Mrs G K James
Huxley
18 Lock Road
MARLOW SL7 1QW
☎ 01628 487741
Fax 01628 890777
Email 101732.2025@compuserve.com

all year 🛏️£25.00 🛏️£19.00 🛏️2 **V**
🚫 👫 over 5 yrs 🚭 DRY ETB 👑 CO

The White House

Mrs E D Durrant
The White House
194 Little Marlow Road
MARLOW SL7 1HX
☎ 01628 485765
Fax 01628 485765

all year 🛏️£30.00 🛏️£25.00 🛏️1 🛏️2
V 🚶🚫 not Sat, Sun 👫 🚭 DRY
ETB 👑👑 CO

Broad Reach

Mrs Pauline King
Broad Reach
Gossmore Lane
MARLOW SL7 1QF
☎ 01628 485735

all year 🛏£30.00 🛏£20.00 🛏2 **V**
🚫 not Sun 👫 🚭 **DRY**

Longridge Scout Boating Centre

Mr G Bucknell
Longridge Scout Boating Centre
Quarry Wood Road
MARLOW SL7 1RE
☎ 01628 483252
Fax 01628 483252
Email longridge@dial.pipex.com

Mar-Oct ⛺ £2.80 ⛺ 20 🚰 🚿
🚿 🍴 🚫 ♿ Youth groups only –
booking essential

MARLOW BOTTOM

⊕ **SU8488** 👢 3km 🚂 Marlow
3.5km 🍴 T J O'Reilly's ✗ ✉
🧺 [||||||||||||] 📞
S M T W T F S

Acorn Lodge Hotel

Mrs Peggy Peers-Johnson
Acorn Lodge Hotel
79 Marlow Bottom
MARLOW SL7 3NA
☎ 01628 472197
Fax 01628 472197

all year 🛏£35.00 🛏£25.00 🛏2
🛏1 **V** Ⓝ not Sun 👫 🚫 🚗
ETB ♕♕ CO

COOKHAM DEAN

⊕ **SU8785** 👢 2.7km cross to south
bank at Marlow or Cookham
🚂 Cookham Rise 2.1km
🍴 several ✗ ✉ 🧺 [||||||||||||]
S M T W T F S
📞

Primrose Hill

Mrs Diana Benson
Primrose Hill
Bradcutts Lane
Cookham Dean
MAIDENHEAD SL6 9TL
☎ 01628 528179

closed Xmas 🛏£20.00 🛏£20.00 🛏1
🛏1 **V** ⚡ Ⓝ not Mon 🏠 👫 🚫
DRY 🚗

Cartlands Cottage

Mr & Mrs R G Parkes
Cartlands Cottage
Kings Lane
Cookham Dean
MAIDENHEAD SL6 9AY
☎ 01628 482196

all year 🛏£22.50 🛏£22.50 🛏1 Ⓝ
👫 🚗 🎁 ETB ♕ AP

TAPLOW

 **SU9082** 1km

Taplow 1.2km S M T W T F S

Cliveden

Mr Stuart Johnson
Cliveden
Taplow
MAIDENHEAD SL6 0JF
☎ 0800 454063 freephone
Fax 0800 454064 freefax

all year £270.00 £135.00 38
V DRY

AA ★★★★★

MAIDENHEAD

SU8981 On the Path **Large town with full range of services**

Maidenhead

Antonio Guest House

Mr G Antinoro
Antonio Guest House
41 Switchback Road North
MAIDENHEAD SL6 7UF
☎ 01628 670537

all year £25.00 £20.00 1
1 1 AA QQ ETB

Ray Corner Guest House

Mrs Maureen Hathaway
Ray Corner Guest House
141 Bridge Road
MAIDENHEAD SL6 8NQ
☎ 01628 632784
Fax 01628 789029

all year £25.00 £20.00 2
1 1 1 V DRY
ETB CO

Copperfields Guest House

Mrs J M Lindsay
Copperfields Guest House
54 Bath Road
MAIDENHEAD SL6 4JY
☎ 01628 674941

all year 🛏£28.00 🛏£22.00 🛏2
🛏3 🚫 📷 👫

Sheephouse Manor

R Street
Sheephouse Manor
Sheephouse Road
MAIDENHEAD SL6 8HJ
☎ 01628 776902
Fax 01628 625138
Email info@sheephousemanor.co.uk

closed Xmas 🛏£35.00 🛏£24.50 🛏1
🛏2 🛏1 V 🚫 📷 👫 🚭 DRY 🎁

Ilex Guest House

Mr Hussain
Ilex Guest House
15 Ray Drive
MAIDENHEAD SL6 8NG
☎ 01628 777229

Fredrick's Hotel & Restaurant

Mrs Kaye Gough
Fredrick's Hotel & Restaurant
Shoppenhangers Road
MAIDENHEAD SL6 2PZ
☎ 01628 635934

Thames Riviera Hotel

Ms Debbie Field
Thames Riviera Hotel
At The Bridge
MAIDENHEAD SL6 8DW
☎ 01628 674057

Walton Cottage Hotel

Mrs England
Walton Cottage Hotel
Marlow Road
MAIDENHEAD SL6 7LT
☎ 01628 624394

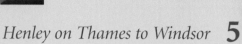

Holiday Inn

Ms Jackie Kelly
Holiday Inn
Manor Lane
MAIDENHEAD SL6 2RA
☎ 01628 623444

Thames Hotel

Mr C Owen
Thames Hotel
Ray Mead Road
MAIDENHEAD SL6 8NR
☎ 01628 628721

Clifton Guest House

The Proprietor
Clifton Guest House
21 Craufurd Rise
MAIDENHEAD SL6 7LR
☎ 01628 623572

Laburnham Guest House

The Proprietor
Laburnham Guest House
31 Laburnham Road
MAIDENHEAD SL6 4DB
☎ 01628 676748

Gables End

Mrs V Blight
Gables End
4 Gables Close
MAIDENHEAD SL6 8QD
☎ 01628 639630

Boulters Lock Hotel

Ms Julie Holton
Boulters Lock Hotel
Boulters Island
MAIDENHEAD SL6 8PE
☎ 01628 621291

Elva Lodge Hotel

The Proprietor
Elva Lodge Hotel
Castle Hill
MAIDENHEAD SL6 4AD
☎ 01628 622948

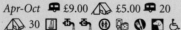

Amerden Caravan & Camping Park

Mrs B Hakesley
Amerden Caravan & Camping Park
Old Marsh Lane
Dorney Reach
MAIDENHEAD SL6 0EE
☎ 01628 627461

Apr-Oct 🚐 £9.00 ⛺ £5.00 🚐 20
⛺ 30 📱 🚿 🔥 ℗ 🛒 🚫 🏞 ♿

ETON

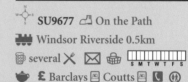

⊕ **SU9677** 🏠 On the Path
🚌 Windsor Riverside 0.5km
🍺 several ✕ ✉ 🏦 | | | | | | | | | | | |
　　　　　　　　　　　　　S M T W T F S
🍵 £ Barclays 🏧 Coutts 🏧 ☎ ♿

The Crown & Cushion

Mrs Sylvia Glinister
The Crown & Cushion
84 High Street
Eton
WINDSOR SL4 6AF
☎ 01753 861531

all year 🛏£29.50 🛏£29.50 🛏5
🛏3 🛏2 V ⚠ 🚫 � **DRY**
ETB **LI CO**

WINDSOR

SU9676 On the Path **Town with full range of services** Windsor

The Laurels

Mrs Joyce
The Laurels
22 Dedworth Road
WINDSOR SL4 5AY
☎ 01753 855821

closed Xmas £25.00 £20.00 1
2 V 🍴 🚭 🖼 †† 🚭 DRY

Mrs V Ford

57 Grove Road
WINDSOR SL4 1JD
☎ 01753 853600

all year £25.00 £22.00 1 🚭
†† 🚭

Arfers

Mrs D W Airey
Arfers
48 Clarence Road
WINDSOR SL4 5AU
☎ 01753 855062
Fax 01753 855062

all year £30.00 £22.50 2
1 V 🚭 †† over 12 years 🚭

Clarence Hotel

The Proprietor
Clarence Hotel
9 Clarence Road
WINDSOR SL4 5AE
☎ 01753 864436
Fax 01753 857060

all year £36.00 £22.50 4
5 6 4 V 🚭 🖼 †† DRY
AA **LI** RAC **LI** ETB **LI** CO

Ms Jean Sumner

1 Stovell Road
WINDSOR SL4 5JB
☎ 01753 852055

all year £40.00 £22.50 1
1 V 🍴 🚭 🚭 🖼 ETB **LI** CO

Fairlight Lodge Hotel

Mr David Stone
Fairlight Lodge Hotel
41 Frances Road
WINDSOR SL4 3AQ
☎ 01753 861207
Fax 01753 865963

all year 🛏 £57.00 🛏 £34.50 🛏 2
🛏 5 🛏 2 🛏 1 V 🔥 🚫 📷 ⚥ 🚭 🎁
ETB 👑👑👑 CO

Oakley Court Hotel

Mrs Catherine Whittle
Oakley Court Hotel
Windsor Road
Water Oakley
WINDSOR SL4 5UR
☎ 01753 609988
Fax 01628 637011
Email oakleyct@atlas.co.uk

all year 🛏 £156.00 🛏 £78.00 🛏 40
🛏 55 🛏 20 V 🔥 🚫 ⚥ ♿ DRY
ETB ★★★★ DL

Langton House

Mr & Mrs P Fogg
Langton House
46 Alma Road
WINDSOR SL4 3HA
☎ 01753 858299

all year 🛏 £27.50 🛏 2 V 🚫 ⚥ 🚫
DRY ETB LI

Windsor Youth Hostel

The Manager
Windsor Youth Hostel
Edgeworth House
Mill Lane
WINDSOR SL4 5JE
☎ 01753 861710
Fax 01753 832100

all year 🛏 £13.25 🔥 🚫

Windsor to Teddington

Section Six

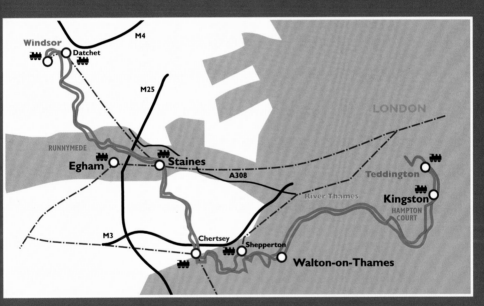

6 Windsor to Teddington

This last non-tidal 39 km of the Thames Path follows a truly Royal Thames from Windsor Castle to beyond Hampton Court with much of interest in between, including Runnymede where the Magna Carta was signed in 1215. Considering the proximity to London there are surprising amounts of pleasant countryside for you to enjoy upstream of Shepperton.

6 A Taster

The famous landmark of Windsor Castle above the Thames is the dramatic start of this section, and from Windsor to another royal town, Kingston, water abounds in all directions. On both sides you'll see gravel-extracted lagoons or the embanked reservoirs holding London's water supply, most bearing royal names.

Inevitably there has been much suburban growth this close to London and you'll come across lots of riverside dwellings, many peeping through the foliage of weeping willows. However, from your initial route through Windsor Castle's Home Park to as far as Shepperton, you'll still find open meadows to complement the built up areas.

From Windsor you reach Datchet, where in the 1830s an old bridge, long since gone, was rebuilt by Berkshire and Buckinghamshire since their county boundaries ran through the centre of the span. Perversely, Berkshire rebuilt their half in iron whilst Buckinghamshire used wood!

Runnymede, of such historic importance, follows before you come to Staines which, until man-made structures were built to impede the river's flow, was the upper limit of the Thames' tidal reach. Staines is ancient but very urban today. Passing the most impressive river loop along the whole Thames at Penton Hook your journey soon takes you onto Shepperton where an alternative route along the north bank is provided for the times when the ferry to take you across the river to Weybridge is not operating.

After a few kilometres the splendours of Hampton Court are reached. Pause before you get to the Palace to look at the bridge which appears to be old and constructed of brick and stone. This was however designed by Sir Edwin Lutyens and built in 1933 of camouflaged concrete. It's just a short distance from Hampton Court Park to Teddington Lock, beyond which the Thames is now tidal, and then you are into London.

Landranger Maps	Explorer Maps	Pathfinder Maps
175 Reading & Windsor	160 Windsor, Weybridge and Bracknell	1173 (SU87/97) Windsor
176 West London	161 London South	1174 (TQ07/17) Staines, Heathrow & Richmond
		1190 (TQ06/16) Weybridge Esher & Hampton Court

Public Transport Information
- National Rail - 24 hours a day   0345 484950
- London Transport Travel Information   0171 2221234
- London 24-hour Travelcheck   0171 2221200
- All London Bus Guide (free leaflet)   0171 371 0247

Police
Surrey	01483 571212
Greater London	0171 230 1212
Thames River Police	0171 928 0333

Hospitals
Isleworth   0181 560 2121
West Middlesex Hospital, Twickenham Road, Isleworth
Hammersmith   0181 846 1234
Charing Cross Hospital, Fulham Palace Road, London W6
Chelsea   0181 746 8000
Chelsea & Westminster Hospital, Fulham Road, London SW6

TOURIST INFORMATION CENTRES

Windsor   24 High Street, Windsor SL4 1LH. Tel 01753 743900 (general information) 01753 743907 (accommodation bookings), fax 01753 743904.
Opening hours   Mon-Sun 10:00-17:00 (subject to seasonal changes)

Kingston upon Thames
     Market House, Market Place, Kingston upon Thames KT1 1JS. Tel 0181 547 5592, fax 0181 547 5594, web site www.rbk.kingston.gov.uk.
Opening hours   All year: Mon-Fri 10:00-17:00, Sat 9:00-16:00

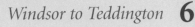

DATCHET

 SU9876 On the Path

Datchet 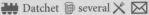 several ✗ ✉

🧺 |S|M|T|W|T|F|S| 🫖

£ Nationwide Building Soc ☎ ♿

The Chimneys

Mrs Margarette Greenham
The Chimneys
55 London Road
Datchet
SLOUGH SL3 9JY
☎ 01753 580401
Fax 01753 540233

closed Xmas, New Year 🛏£28.50
🛏 £25.00 🛏 1 🛏 1 🛏 1 **V** 🚫 not
Sun 🚷 🚭

EGHAM

TO0171 On the Path **Town
with full range of services** Egham

Runnymede Hotel

Ms Louise Martin
Runnymede Hotel
Windsor Road
EGHAM TW20 0AG
☎ 01784 436171
Fax 01784 436340
Email info@runnymedehotel.com

all year 🛏£77.95 🛏 £62.90 🛏14
🛏 131 🛏 35 **V** 🔥 🚫 🚷 ♿
AA ★★★★ RAC ★★★★
ETB 👑👑👑👑👑 HC

STAINES

✛ **TO0371** ⛺ On the Path **Large town with full range of services**

🚂 Staines

The Penton

Mrs Isabel Kelly
The Penton
39 Penton Road
STAINES TW18 2JX
☎ 01784 458787

all year 🛏£20.00 🛏£22.50 🛏2
🛏1 🛏1 🛏1 V 🚫 ♀♂

Albany House

Mrs Patricia Norbury
Albany House
2 Glebe Road
STAINES TW18 1BX
☎ 01784 441223
Fax 01784 444413

all year 🛏£29.00 🛏£22.50 🛏1
🛏1 🛏1 🛏1 V 🚫 ♀♂ **DRY**

The Thames Lodge Hotel

Mr Peter Watt
The Thames Lodge Hotel
Thames Street
STAINES TW18 4SF
☎ 01784 464433
Fax 01784 454858

all year 🛏£45.00 🛏£45.00 🛏7
🛏42 🛏11 🛏19 V 🏕 🚫 🖻 ♀♂
♿ 🗑 AA ★★★

Laleham Camping Club

Mrs Berbridge
Laleham Camping Club
Thameside
LALEHAM TW18 1SH
☎ 01932 564149

Apr-Sep 🚐£5.50 ⛺£4.00 🚐30
⛺100 🔲 🔥 🔥 🚻 🖾 🚫 🖻 ♿ **DRY**

SHEPPERTON

TO0867 On the Path **Town**
with full range of services
Shepperton

Splash Cottage

Mr & Mrs M Shaw
Splash Cottage
91 Watersplash Road
SHEPPERTON TW17 0EE
☎ 01932 229987

all year £21.00 £17.00 2
1 V 🔥 🚫 👬 🚭 🚗 🛏

Ship Hotel

Mr Chris Plumpton
Ship Hotel
Russell Road
SHEPPERTON TW17 9HX
☎ 01932 227320
Fax 01932 226668

all year £37.00 £30.00 14
14 3 V 🔥 🚫 👬 ♿ **DRY** 🛏

Warren Lodge Hotel

Mr Gavin Baragwanath
Warren Lodge Hotel
Church Square
SHEPPERTON TW17 9JZ
☎ 01932 242972
Fax 01932 253883
Email 106346.3471@compuserve.com

all year £37.50 £37.50 8
34 4 2 V 🔥 🚫 👬
RAC ★★★ ETB 👑👑👑 CO

WALTON-ON-THAMES

TO1066 On the Path **Town**
with full range of services
Walton-on-Thames

Beech Tree Lodge

Mrs Joan Spiteri
Beech Tree Lodge
7 Rydens Avenue
WALTON-ON-THAMES KT12 3JB
☎ 01932 242738
Fax 01932 886667

all year £22.00 £18.00 1 2
1 V 🔥 🚫 👬 🚭 **DRY**
ETB **LI CO**

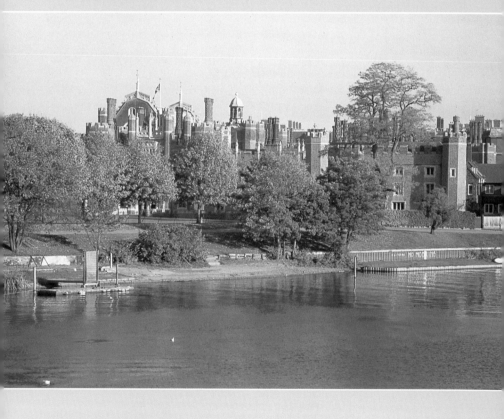

KINGSTON UPON THAMES

TO1869  On the Path **Town with full range of services**

Kingston

Mrs Heather Logue

16 Chivenor Grove
Royal Park Gate
KINGSTON upon THAMES KT2 5GE
☎ 0181 547 0074
Fax 0181 547 0074

all year £40.00 £20.00 1 **V**

Abollon

The Proprietor
Abollon
46 Milner Road
KINGSTON upon THAMES KT1 2AV
☎ 0181 255 3992

Mrs M Askey

95 Wolsey Drive
KINGSTON upon THAMES KT2 5DR
☎ 0181 549 2529

Mrs Sylvia Calvert

2 Clifton Road
KINGSTON upon THAMES KT2 6PW
☎ 0181 549 2269

Mrs Dawson

62 Gloucester Road
Norbiton
KINGSTON upon THAMES KT1 3RB
☎ 0181 546 0433

Mrs P Hulbert

281A Richmond Road
KINGSTON upon THAMES KT2 5DJ
☎ 0181 546 7389

Hermes Hotel & Crowleys Restaurant

The Proprietor
Hermes Hotel & Crowleys Restaurant
1 Portsmouth Road
KINGSTON upon THAMES
☎ 0181 546 5322

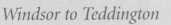

Hotel Antoinette of Kingston

The Proprietor
Hotel Antoinette of Kingston
26 Beaufort Road
KINGSTON upon THAMES KT1 2TQ
☎ 0181 546 1044

The Grecian Hotel

Mr Mallinson
The Grecian Hotel
12 Lingfield Avenue
KINGSTON upon THAMES KT1 2TN
☎ 0181 546 2719

Mrs Lefebvre

40 The Bittoms
KINGSTON upon THAMES KT1 2AP
☎ 0181 541 3171

Ms Pat Lockwood

36 Latchmere Road
KINGSTON upon THAMES
☎ 0181 549 0474

TEDDINGTON

✛ **TO1671** ⛺ On the Path **Town**
with full range of services
🚂 Teddington

Bushy Park Lodge

Mr Martin Bosher
Bushy Park Lodge
6 Sandy Lane
TEDDINGTON TW11 0DR
☎ 0181 943 5428
Fax 0181 943 1917
Email bosher@btinternet.com

all year 🛏 £49.00 🛏 £29.50 🛏 6
🛏 6 🚫 👬 ♿ **DRY** 🚗 🎁

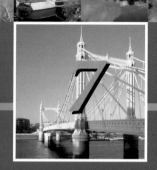

Teddington to Westminster

Section Seven

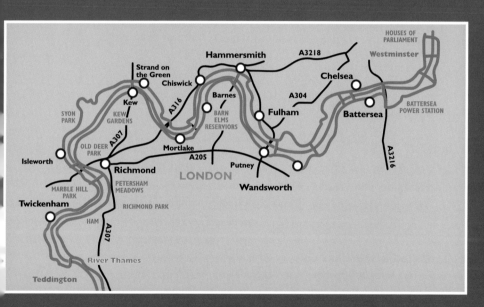

HOUSES OF
PARLIAMENT

Westminster

A3218

Hammersmith

Chelsea

Strand on
the Green

Chiswick

A304

Kew

Barnes

Fulham

Battersea

BATTERSEA
POWER STATION

SYON
PARK

KEW
GARDENS

A316

BARN
ELMS
RESERVIORS

A3216

OLD DEER
PARK

A307

Mortlake

A205

Putney

Isleworth

Richmond

LONDON

Wandsworth

MARBLE HILL
PARK

PETERSHAM
MEADOWS

Twickenham

RICHMOND PARK

HAM

A307

River Thames

Teddington

7 LONDON: Teddington to Westminster

You can choose to walk on either the south (32 km) or north (34 km) bank
of the river as you head into the heart of London on this section. You'll find
surprising amounts of greenery at the start, some impressive historic
houses on both banks and old village settlements now absorbed by the city.

Whether you walk on the south or north bank, or cross from one side to the other where bridges allow, there's a tremendous amount to see between Teddington and Westminster.

The first few kilometres of this section are remarkably rural as you pass through Ham Lands, Petersham Meadows, Richmond's Old Deer Park and Kew Gardens on the south, and through Marble Hill Park and Syon Park on the north. Best views of the looping river can be seen from Richmond Hill and you'll be in good company if you make the detour since many famous poets, writers and artists have been inspired from this spot for centuries.

Strand on the Green on the north bank is a miraculously preserved riverside community with picturesque fishermen's cottages and elegant period houses overlooking the river. Other old settlements like Richmond, Kew, Barnes, Hammersmith, Fulham and Putney still also manage to retain some flavour of village atmosphere.

From Chiswick and Mortlake to Westminster, the river is wholly urban in character but trees and bushes grow at the water's edge creating almost a linear park. Mortlake is the finish of the annual spring Varsity Boat Race between Oxford and Cambridge Universities which has been held since 1845 and starts downstream at Putney. At Barn Elms waterworks, the reservoirs are being transformed into natural looking lakes and ponds to attract a range of birds and other wildlife into the heart of London.

Elegant and expensive Chelsea on the north bank has been home for many famous literary and artistic people. Standing in Chelsea you'll look across the river to Battersea, your view dominated by the 1936 power station, now just an empty shell. Battersea used to be known for its asparagus beds, but most people now associate it with its dogs' home.

Your finish to this section could hardly be more impressive since you either stop outside or look across to the Houses of Parliament in Westminster, the seat of government.

Public Transport Information
- London Transport Travel Information 0171 222 1234
- www.londontransport.co.uk
- boat trips 0839 123 432

Police

Surrey	01483 571212
Greater London	0171 230 1212
Thames River Police	0171 928 0333

Hospitals

Isleworth 0181 560 2121
West Middlesex Hospital, Twickenham Road, Isleworth
Hammersmith 0181 846 1234
Charing Cross Hospital, Fulham Palace Road, London W6
Chelsea 0181 746 8000
Chelsea & Westminster Hospital, Fulham Road, London SW6

Landranger Maps	Explorer Maps	Pathfinder Maps
176 West London	161 London South	1174 (TQ07/17) Staines, Heathrow & Richmond 1175 (TQ27/37) Wimbledon & Dulwich

TOURIST INFORMATION CENTRES

Richmond   Old Town Hall, Whittaker Avenue, Richmond
                        TW9 1TP. Tel 0181 940 9125, fax 0181 940 6899.

Opening hours   Summer: (May 1-Oct 31) Mon-Fri 10:00-18:00, Sat
                        10:00-17:00, Sun 10:15-16:15. Winter: (Nov 1-Apr
                        30) Mon-Fri 10:00-18:00, Sat 10:00-17:00

Britain Visitor Centre 1 Lower Regent Street, London SW1 4XT (personal
                        callers only).

Opening hours   All year: Mon-Fri 9:00-18:30, Sat-Sun 10:00-16:00

London Tourist Board   Victoria Station (personal callers only). For
                        accommodation bookings: Tel 0171 932 2020
                        'Credit Card Booking Service' – no general enquiries.

LONDON

Oxford Street Youth Hostel

The Manager
Oxford Street Youth Hostel
14 Noel Street
LONDON W1V 3PD
☎ 0171 734 1618
Fax 0171 734 1657

🛏 £19.45 no breakfasts

Earl's Court Youth Hostel

The Manager
Earl's Court Youth Hostel
38 Bolton Gardens
LONDON SW5 0AQ
☎ 0171 373 7083
Fax 0171 835 2034

🛏 £19.45

Hampstead Heath Youth Hostel

The Manager
Hampstead Heath Youth Hostel
4 Wellgarth Road
Golders Green
LONDON NW11 7HR
☎ 0181 458 9054
Fax 0181 209 0546

🛏 £19.45

Holland House Youth Hostel

The Manager
Holland House Youth Hostel
Holland Walk
Kensington
LONDON W8 7QU
☎ 0171 937 0748
Fax 0171 376 0667

🛏 £19.45

Westminster to Thames Barrier

Section Eight

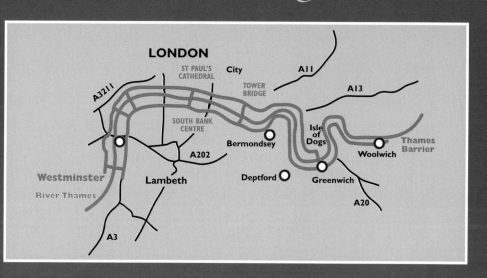

8 LONDON: Westminster to Thames Barrier

This last section is relatively short, 19 km if you keep to the north bank or 18 km if you walk on the south side. Short it may be, but it's packed with the fascinating history of London. The Thames Path keeps next to the river wherever possible, but beyond Tower Bridge the banks used to be crammed solid with wharves and warehouses so that in places the Path currently has to detour away from the river.

8 A Taster

So much to see and to explore in such a short distance! Too much, too, to give you anything here but a flavour of the London you'll be walking through. But, of course, there are numerous guide books about London for you to choose from and you can visit the London Tourist Board website at www.londontown.com

Your route from Westminster to the fabulous Tower Bridge on the north bank of the Thames is rich in the history of England's capital city. You'll pass, amongst other places, Whitehall, Cleopatra's Needle, the Inns of Court, the square mile of the City of London, St Paul's Cathedral, the Monument, London Bridge, several historic ships moored on the river and the Tower of London; all in just 4km.

On the opposite bank, along the same section, you're route takes in the almost French atmosphere of the promenade beneath the National Theatre, great views of the City and St Paul's across the river, the massive brick former power station at Bankside, Shakespeare's recently reconstructed Globe Theatre and Francis Drake's schooner the Golden Hind.

From Tower Bridge to the finish (or start) of the Thames Path at the Thames Barrier in Woolwich you'll be walking through the old heart of the working river. On the south bank you'll also pass Greenwich, where east and west meet either side of the meridian line and where the Millennium Dome is sited. In places the riverside is still crowded with decaying piers, wharves, warehouses and other paraphernalia of shipping, and there are still a few lighters and barges on the Thames. But the docks, mostly built in the 19th century to cope with the huge amount of ships unloading and loading their cargoes, are now redundant. Since the 1980s much of this landscape has been transformed by development, but there are still hidden corners for you to find and where you can try to imagine what it was like when London was the busiest port in the world.

Landranger Maps	Explorer Maps	Pathfinder Maps
176 West London 177 East London	173 London North	1175 (TQ27/37) Wimbledon & Dulwich 1159 (TQ28/38) City of London 1176 (TQ47/57) Bexley & Dartford

Public Transport Information
- London Transport Travel Information 0171 222 1234
- www.londontransport.co.uk
- boat trips 0839 123 432

Police
Greater London 0171 230 1212

Thames River Police 0171 928 0333

Hospitals
Lambeth 0171 928 9292

St Thomas' Hospital, Lambeth Palace Road, London SE1

The City 0171 955 5000

Guy's Hospital, St Thomas Street, London SE1

Dartford 01322 227242

Joyce Green Hospital, Joyce Green Lane, Dartford

TOURIST INFORMATION CENTRES

Britain Visitor Centre	1 Lower Regent Street, London SW1 4XT (personal callers only).
Opening hours	All year: Mon-Fri 9:00-18:30, Sat-Sun 10:00-16:00
London Tourist Board	Victoria Station (personal callers only). For accommodation bookings: Tel 0171 932 2020 'Credit Card Booking Service' – no general enquiries.
City of London Information Centre	St Paul's Churchyard, London EC4M 8BX. Tel 0171 332 1456, fax 0171 332 1457 (no accommodation information).
Opening hours	Summer: (Apr 1-Sep 30) daily 9:30-17:00 Winter: (Oct 1-Mar 31) Mon-Fri 9:30-17:00, Sat 9:30-12:30
Southwark	Lower Level, Cotton's Centre, Middle Yard, London SE1 2QJ. Tel 0171 403 8299 (situated in Hay's Galleria).
Opening hours	All year: daily 10:00-17:00
Greenwich	46 Greenwich Church Street, Greenwich, London SE10 9BL. Tel 0181 858 6376, fax 0181 853 4607
Opening hours	Daily 10:00-17:00 (subject to seasonal changes).

Tent City East Acton

Ms Maxine Lambert
Tent City East Acton
Old Oak Common Lane
East Acton
LONDON W3 7DP
☎ 0181 743 5708
Fax 0181 749 9074
Email tentcity@btinternet.com

Jun-Sep 🚐 £6.00 ⛺ £6.00 🚐 30
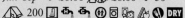 200 🗐 🐓 🐓 ⓗ ⓞ 🍽 🛶 🚳 **DRY**

St Pancras International Youth Hostel

The Manager
St Pancras International Youth Hostel
Euston Road
LONDON N1
☎ 0171 248 6547
Fax 0171 236 7681

🛏 £22.15

City of London Youth Hostel

The Manager
City of London Youth Hostel
36 Carter Lane
LONDON EC4V 5AB
☎ 0171 236 4965
Fax 0171 236 7681

🛏 £22.15

Rotherhithe Youth Hostel

The Manager
Rotherhithe Youth Hostel
Salter Road
LONDON SE16 1PP
☎ 0171 232 2114
Fax 0171 237 2919

🛏 £22.15

Tent City Hackney

Ms Maxine Lambert
Tent City Hackney
Millfields Road
Hackney
LONDON E5 0AB
☎ 0181 985 7656
Fax 0181 749 9074
Email tentcity@btinternet.com

Jun - Sep 🚐 £5.00 ⛺ £5.00 🚐 30
⛺ 150 ▯ ♨ ♨ Ⓦ ▣ ▨ ♨ ♨
DRY

INDEX OF PLACES